THE MOMENT OF
CHRISTIAN WITNESS

HANS URS VON BALTHASAR

The Moment of Christian Witness

Translated by
Richard Beckley

IGNATIUS PRESS   SAN FRANCISCO

Title of the German original:
Cordula oder der Ernstfall
© 1966, 1987 Johannes Verlag, Einsiedeln, Trier
Published with ecclesiastical permission
Translation © 1969 by The Missionary Society of
St. Paul the Apostle in the State of New York

Cover design by Roxanne Mei Lum

Published in 1994 by Ignatius Press, San Francisco
ISBN 978-0-89870-516-4
Library of Congress catalogue number 94-75997
Printed in the United States of America

Contents

Preface

In the following pages I make a proposal and submit it to Christians for their consideration. A criterion is offered, and indeed a better one. Better than what? This use of the unrelated comparative is well known in the advertising world. "Brand X washes whiter"— whiter than what? To say more might lead to legal complications with other soap manufacturers. It would, moreover, be a tactical mistake in the art of salesmanship, because the unrelated comparative is more stimulating and evocative in its effect than the related comparative. And on this occasion something a little more evocative is what is required.

A criterion has a stimulating effect, even if one uses it only in a purely experimental way to exercise one's imagination. If you say to Georges Bernanos, "Come along with me. It's the *Ernstfall*—the crucial moment in Christian experience", the old grumbler will get up out of his armchair without so much as raising an eyebrow and follow you like a lamb. But if you go to Reinhold Schneider, the author of *Winter in Vienna*, and say the same thing to him, there is no telling what might happen. Whether you would finally manage to get any response at all from those who have been "demythologized" and converted to the world, I do not know. They have already explained everything away and are left with a merely symbolic belief in a message that they understand only by analogy. For them, both the belief and the message are worth dying for only by analogy, just as they consider their Christianity worth living for only by analogy to something else.

However, let us take this lantern of Diogenes and see what can be done with its help. Perhaps by its light we shall distinguish between people who otherwise look very much alike from the outside. One of these may be burning with love, and in his eyes every means may seem right that will help him to speak in a new way of love of Christ to someone who is hard to convince in this respect. But another may secretly feel that he has heard enough about the gospel, the Cross and the whole business about dogma and the sacraments, because he senses something new in the air. He may be out to kill two birds with one stone; in an unexpected and unforeseen manner he may find he can get rid of several things that have been thoroughly ruined for him, and at the same time be able to march forward as an enlightened and reformed Christian, in line with the latest learning, toward a better future. One person will demythologize in order to arrive at a purer and deeper faith; another will do it in order not to have to believe anything at all any longer.

The present state of Christianity conceals as much ambiguity as ever it did in the past! Therefore, let us take the lantern and perhaps we shall find among the great number of those who profess to be Christians a few who genuinely are! For who knows if, when the show actually begins, there may not be quite a few who will gladly step up onto the stage and take the part of a Genesius or a Cordula?

I

The Decisive Moment

Since Jesus, the Son of God, manifested his charity by laying down his life for us, no one has greater love than he who lays down his life for Christ and his brothers (cf. 1 Jn 3:6; Jn 15:13). From the earliest times, then, some Christians have been called upon—and some will always be called upon—to give this supreme testimony of love to all men, but especially to persecutors. The Church therefore considers martyrdom as an exceptional gift and as the highest proof of love.

By martyrdom a disciple is transformed into an image of his master who freely accepted death on behalf of the world's salvation; he perfects that image even to the shedding of blood. Though few are presented with such an opportunity, nevertheless all must be prepared to confess Christ before men, and to follow him along the way of the cross through the persecutions which the Church will never fail to suffer.

—Vatican II, *Lumen Gentium*
Dogmatic Constitution on the Church

1. *The Scriptural Basis*

Why was it that Jesus Christ prophesied no other fate for his disciples and followers than his own: persecution, failure and suffering to the point of death? It is true that the great speech with which he sends them out into the world at the end of St. Matthew's Gospel, and which is splendidly phrased in words inspired by the Holy Spirit, entrusts them with a commission of universal significance for all times and places and for all civilizations, both present and future. A commission, however, does not of itself constitute a guarantee that it will be carried through to its completion. It often happens that the greatest achievements of humanity are those that fill us with a vision of immense possibilities but break off before these possibilities are realized. It is true, moreover, that a commission of this kind makes such a super-human demand on our strength that the prospect of our having to undergo suffering, or even to fulfill it partially, is never very far away. This is especially true when one considers that Christians are said to be sent out among wolves—a frightful image, if one takes the trouble to think for a moment what it really signifies: not only the helplessness and defenselessness of the lamb, but also the natural and therefore insatiable and ineradicable bloodthirstiness of the wolf. The great messianic speech in Matthew 10, which contains detailed instructions for putting into practical effect the inspired vision of Matthew 28:19–20, takes advantage of the sheep-wolf imagery as an occasion for a parallel series of statements interwoven one with another. One series is preceded by the warning "Beware!" and contains the darkest prophecies of coming persecutions in Matthew 10, verses 17–18, 21–22 and 34–36. The other series belongs together with the exhortation "So have no fear of them!" and contains the most joyful promises of victory in verses 19–20, 26, 28, 31 and 40–42.

The one series seems to be a clear contradiction of the other. For the situation of death is each time either implicit or explicit in the warnings. It is already implicit in the sheep-wolf imagery. If we do not feel it is expressed unambiguously enough in the incidents in which Christ is delivered up to the judgment of ecclesiastical courts and to scourgings, or is led before governors and kings, John makes it clear for us when he writes: "Whoever kills you will think he is offering service to God" (Jn 16:2), while in Matthew 10:12 *paradosis* is clearly described as being delivered up to death: "Brother will deliver up brother to death, and the father his child, and children will rise against parents and have them put to death." Here the concern is with the death of the body as opposed to the death of the soul, since God alone has the power to consign us to damnation. The sword that divides men (Mt 10:34ff.) does not diminish the danger of death; on the contrary, it reveals the conditions preexistent within the situation, the likelihood of their extent: hate (Mt 10:22; Jn 15:18) and the unendurable pain of acknowledging Christ (*martyrion*: Mt 10:18, cf. 32–33). But whereas the series of warnings clearly speaks of the situation of death, the series of promises seems to exclude each of them: "But he who endures to the end will be saved" (Mt 10:22). Even the sparrows are in the care of the Father; how much more so, therefore, are those who acknowledge his Son (Mt 10:29–31).

It is as if the Lord were not concerned here with a contradiction, and even less with the resolving of a contradiction, for the position from which he speaks, and from which springs the series of interwoven and unifying statements that make the speech intelligible when seen as a whole, is the position in which he is actually placed. One may go further and say it is the position that he represents and that exists only because he is in it. The idea contained in "If the world hates you, know that it has hated me before it hated you" is clarified by John when he refers expressly to the speech in Matthew in which Christ sends his disciples out into the world: "Remember the Word that I said to you, 'A servant is not greater than his master.' If they persecuted me, they will persecute you" (Jn 15:18, 20). When recalled to memory by Matthew, this saying has something almost showy in its expansiveness: "A disciple is not above his teacher, nor a servant above his master; it is enough for the disciple to be like his teacher, and the servant like his master. If they have called the master of the house Beelzebub, how much more will they malign those of his household" (Mt 10:24–25). This "how much more" with its heightening effect may be disturbing, for one would imagine that, after what has been said about the master-disciple relationship, it is hardly possible that Christ's followers could ever attain to his position of eminence. But in this instance Christ's position is unfortunately more than attained, for if "they hated me without cause" (Jn 15:25), then it will be your highest honor to "be hated by all for my name's sake" (Mt 10:22), even if there is cause enough to hate you for other reasons and to call you servants of the house of Beelzebub.

However, it is not this that stands out so much as the final utterance, which gives the key to the whole speech: "He who loves father or mother more than me is not worthy of me; and he who does not take up his cross and follow me is not worthy of me. He who finds his life will lose it, and he who loses his life for my sake will find it" (Mt 10:37–39). Here it becomes clear that the warning against the "wolves" ("Beware of men": Mt 10:17) does not refer simply to a possible situation, but to an inevitable one, because in the absolute decision to follow Christ one is exposed to the counterdecision of "the hate of the world".

Why is this so? One could argue that the tensions between "a man and his father, a daughter and her mother, a daughter-in-law and her mother-in-law" (Mt 10:35) do not necessarily have to end in this hostile way; in a tolerant and pluralistic universe they may be settled amicably by the mutual adoption of

an attitude of "live and let live". Who knows? Perhaps this is another of those numerous instances in
which present-day Christianity may have evolved
beyond the aims of its founder. Unfortunately, however, its founder has cut short this dream of advance-
ment beyond his aims (Mt 10:25), and likewise that
of "peaceful coexistence", by declaring his historical
"Cross" (Mt 10:38) to be an eternal one, and by
making it the permanent pattern of the lives of those
who willingly follow him. Those who willingly follow Christ put him first, regarding him as "worth
more" than "father and mother, son and daughter"
(Mt 10:37), but who puts Jesus first chooses the Cross
as the place where he will not eventually but most
certainly die.

Seen in this light, the concluding passage illuminates the paradox of the whole speech: "He who
finds his life will lose it." A man may demand, as a
conditio sine qua non, that he, his family, his friends, his
career, his concern for the people, the state, civiliza-
tion, the world, the present and the future (*mellonta*:
Rom 8:38) be placed on an equal footing with
Christ. He does so under the pretext that these are
all-good, God-created things and that the order of
redemption cannot possibly contradict the order of
creation, since God himself strives for a synthesis of
the two; in his eyes, man therefore probably has the
right, perhaps even the duty, to do the same, for the
very reason that the order of redemption distinctly

tells us to care for all these things, particularly our fellow men. Such a man will lose his life in whatever way this expression is meant to be understood, whether as a life surrounded by all these valuable earthly goods and to the exclusion of Christ, or—what really amounts to the same thing—as a life surrounded by these goods but with the additional attempt to establish a self-decreed synthesis between these and the commands of Christ. In the first case a man will lose his life at the very latest when physical death overtakes him. In the second case, however, the loss of life will be more painful and profound, because the self-decreed synthesis is dead, in the sense of being bad and unfruitful, and neither a proper worldly life nor a proper Christian life can be led according to its principles. "For whoever loses his life for my sake will find it" (cf. Mt 16:25; Mt 8:34–35; Lk 17:33). The words "for my sake" represent the dividing line, the "sword" (Mt 10:34) that produces, out of itself as it were, the unexpected reconciliation and synthesis. The man who stakes his all on this one thing wins all, but he must of course reckon with the loss of everything else excluded by this one thing.

The underlying idea of Christ's speech is the Cross; it is both the point of departure for his argument and the goal toward which he expressly invites his followers to strive. It has here become a matter of indifference whether we are speaking of the loss of all earthly things, including life, or of the unexpected preservation, final salvation and rest in the bosom of the Father. Both have become so much one and the same thing that it is no longer important how the idea is expressed. The point at which life comes forth out of death is in Jesus Christ and in ourselves through him, and the Holy Spirit proceeds from the giving back of the spirit to the Father. "When they deliver you up, do not be anxious how you are to speak or what you are to say; for what you are to say will be given to you in that hour; for it is not you who speak, but the spirit of your Father speaking through you" (Mt 10:19–20).

Josef Schmid summarizes the contents of this speech with beautiful simplicity: "The leading idea is that suffering in its manifold forms—being parted from one's dearest friends, being persecuted and finally martyred—is intrinsic to the fate of the disciples. That this is so has its cause in the person of Christ who forces man to decide for or against this fate. In his person and through his Word he is the revelation of God, which no one can therefore ignore. For this reason those who confess his name cannot avoid drawing upon themselves the hate of all other men. *For his name's sake* they will be hated by all (Mt 10:22). This means that it is not human misunderstanding but a divinely ordained necessity that creates martyrs. Martyrdom, by means of which the hate of the 'world' for the disciples on the one hand

and discipleship on the other achieve completion, has its roots in the person of Christ and in the gospels that act as an irritant in the world. But just as no one can become a disciple of Christ who is not called to the task by Christ himself, so men do not become martyrs out of personal conviction or the zeal of their belief. Christ himself calls men to martyrdom, and it is this that makes it a special sign of grace. For this reason the declarations that a martyr may make before public authorities or representatives of the State are not simply declarations of personal conviction, but words spoken by the Holy Spirit through someone who professes faith in Christ (Mt 10:20)." [1]

2. The Ernstfall as the Form of the Christian Life

According to this speech made by Christ, persecution constitutes the normal condition of the Church in her relation to the world, and martyrdom is the normal condition of the professed Christian. This does not mean that the Church will necessarily be persecuted at all times and in all places, but if it does happen at certain times and in certain places, then it should be remembered that this is a sign of that special grace promised to her: "But I have said these things to you, that when their hour comes you may

[1] *Das Evangelium nach Matthäus übersetzt und erklärt von J. Schmid* (Regensburg, 1956).

remember that I told you of them" (Jn 16:4). The truth of such words cannot be outdated or superseded by any development in the state of the world. Again, this does not mean that every single Christian must suffer bloody martyrdom, but he must consider the entire case as the external representation of the inner reality out of which he lives. Martyrdom provides a horizon for the Christian life in quite a different sense from the similar position it held in the Jewish faith. In the latter it represented the extreme opportunity within the realm of the humanly possible for the individual believer to prove his belief in Yahweh. Its most striking characteristic is courage in the cause of faith, and the models offered to the whole nation and to youth in particular as examples of this attitude are models of heroism, such as the two women who circumcise their children in defiance of the edict of Antiochus Epiphanes, or Eleazar and the seven brothers (2 Macc 6–7), or Daniel and his friends (Dan 3; 6; 14:31ff.).

It must be borne in mind, however, that the great prophets are expressly called by God to provoke failure: "Make the heart of this people fat, and their ears heavy" (Is 6:10; cf. Jer 1:17–19; Ezek 2:7–9). They are therefore called upon to bear a witness that contains within itself a form of crucifixion for them.

In the New Testament this heroic element disappears, since man no longer needs to advance toward this extreme point, but is seen rather as originating

from a point that Christ has already reached. Christ
has already fulfilled the prophecies concerning the
servant of God, which were a promise of his coming.
There is therefore no longer any need for a continua-
tion of the Old Testament situation for mankind, but
only an entering into the situation of Christ. Whereas
martyrdom in the Old Testament illustrates how
strong the faith of a Jew ought to be, martyrdom in
the New Testament reveals that such a faith, founded
on the crucifixion of Christ and imparted by grace to
his followers, is already real and existent.

Paul puts it in this way (at first without any explanation): "For the love of Christ controls us, because
we are convinced that one has died for all." The
explanation and the grounds for this statement do not
appear until the following verse: "And he died for
all, that those who live might live no longer for
themselves but for him who for their sake died and
was raised" (2 Cor 5:14–15). Christ's dying for us is
presented as an *a priori* of the Christian attitude,
which is thereby stamped as perfect. In the Epistle to
the Romans Paul shows that this objective *a priori*
element in Christ's action has its effect on Christian
baptism, which, independently of any subjective
belief, objectively postulates a state of being dead and
buried with Christ. He then, of course, goes on to
say that the existential attitude of the Christian
should be shaped and determined by this *a priori* element (Rom 6:3–11). Paul's mysterious words in the

Epistle to the Galatians—"For I through the law died to the law that I might live to God. I have been crucified with Christ"—base their argument on the level of this *a priori*, namely, on the level of that which is the objective precondition and form for a faith to be achieved at some subsequent date. Because one died for all, he has brought us all, including me, to his Cross, so that all, including me, are dead to the law and the world in which this law is valid. And when Paul then continues: "It is no longer I who live, but Christ who lives in me", the basis of his statement lies somewhere in the middle between the objective precondition and the subjective achievement of faith, at the point where the Christian acknowledges the fact that someone has been crucified for him. This acknowledgment is simply called belief: "And the life I now live in the flesh, I live by faith in the Son of God who loved me and gave himself for me" (Gal 2:19–20).

We are able to grasp here, in the childlike freshness of its *living* source, what faith, and a life lived through faith, has to tell us. It tells us that we should be thankful with the whole of our being that we owe our whole being to the historical figure of Christ. And since the only reason that I owe my whole being to him is because he sacrificed his being for mine, the only way to express my thanks is with my whole being. The unfortunate thing about Christianity for most of us is that there is no easier means to express thanks than in this way. Why should this be so? Is it not equally conceivable that we could gratefully accept a favor from God (a favor, however, for which God had to pledge the life of his immortal Son) that we did not actually ask for, without having to become so seriously committed on our side? Surely God could be satisfied with a feeling of sincere gratitude on the part of the redeemed who acknowledge their pleasure in the gift received and are even prepared to be constantly and joyfully mindful of the benefit bestowed on them. And surely it would be all the more possible for God to do so, since his act of salvation has already been performed, and nothing decisive or primarily effective can be added to it by such a frightful commitment on the part of mankind. How could there be anything lacking or incomplete about the suffering of Christ? And is not Paul exaggerating when he asserts that what is lacking in Christ's afflictions can be completed by our sufferings (Col 1:24)?

But God does not content himself with our heartfelt thanks. He wants to be able to recognize his own Son in Christian men and women. However far they may fall short of the ideal of Christ in their way of thinking, they must in principle have given their assent to the love by which they have been redeemed. But to assent means to find that this love is *perfectly right*, that it is in fact the only thing that *is* perfectly right. Yet it is also the greatest revelation of divine love, and therefore the norm of all truth, because God is truth. For this reason (which Christians understand) no other norm of truth is valid. They cannot satisfy God with any love or truth other than that which he has accorded to them. And if one looks deeper into the matter they are not even in a position to decide in what existential coin they are prepared to repay God. For if "one has died for all and therefore all have died" (2 Cor 5:14), God has from the outset made a decree concerning the death of all, on the assumption that the greatest revelation of divine love and truth manifested in the death of Christ was perhaps worthy of being considered by man himself as the best prospect earthly life afforded him as the greatest revelation he himself could make to God—and consequently as what must be chosen unconditionally in freedom. In this case a believer would simply be one who has understood this prospect rightly and makes the right use of it. He must either be this or nothing at all. He cannot be one who measures with two different yardsticks, one for God and Christ and one for himself.

The truth that provides the yardstick for faith is God's willingness to die for the world he loves, for mankind and for me as an individual. This love became manifest in the dark night of Christ's crucifixion. Every source of grace—faith, love, and hope—springs from this night. Everything that I am (insofar as I am anything more on this earth than a

fugitive figure without hope, all of whose illusions
are rendered worthless by death), I am solely by virtue of Christ's death, which opens up to me the possibility of fulfillment in God. I blossom on the grave
of God who died for me. I sink my roots deep into
the nourishing soil of his flesh and blood. The love
that I draw in faith from this soil can be of no other
kind than the love of one who is buried.

Christian belief means the unconditional resolve to
surrender one's life for Christ's sake. Just as the triune
God acquired an ascendancy over the God in one
person through an unfathomable love that itself had
to be founded on love (for he did not need us), and,
as a result, fell from eternal life into the world of
death and was forsaken by God, so Christian belief
can be only an ascendancy that man, responding
gratefully and showing himself thankful to God,
acquires over himself by giving evidence that he has
understood God's action.

From a purely superficial point of view this might
appear to be no more than the adoption of the idea
that, when faced with death, man philosophizes with
death as his horizon, for in his conscious anticipation
of death he represents world-transcending spirit. But
in the realm of Christian belief the situation is quite
different. The death of Christ is for us the opening-
up of the glory of divine love, and to understand our
position as believers in the light of this death means
to interpret our position as arising not from a mar-

ginal or borderline situation but from the absolute
center of reality. This does not alter the fact that man
cannot find refuge and security in this center other
than by coming into contact with it through the
marginal or borderline situation of his own death,
and attempting to understand the seriousness of
God's love through the seriousness of this situation.

The anticipation of one's own death as a response
to the death of Christ is the way in which we can lay
certain hold on our faith. If faith means giving God's
truth ascendancy over our own truth—with all its
knowledge, doubt, ignorance, uncertainty and reservations—then our chosen mode of existence above
and beyond any human and therefore doubtful
knowledge of the truth that we may personally possess is the possible proof for us that we give God's
truth the ascendancy over our own. That this truth is
synonymous with love does not require any special
proof. Christ's words, "Greater love has no man than
this, that a man lay down his life for his friends" (Jn
15:13), express a basic and general human truth intelligible to everyone. But this truth here becomes a
boundless mystery by virtue of the fact that the Son
of God claims it for his own and permits us, his followers and disciples, to use it as a key to our self-
understanding as Christians.

Consequently an existence in faith would be one
in the death of love—not an arbitrary sacrifice or surrender varying in degree according to our estimation

of it at any given moment, nor one that we manipulate to suit ourselves, but a willingness in advance to surrender ourselves wholly at every single moment in our Christian existence when the need arises. "By this we know love, that he laid down his life for us, and we ought to lay down our lives for the brethren" (1 Jn 3:16). In this axiom of the beloved disciple, "love" means the absolute love as it appeared in the mystery made manifest by Christ. It comprehends within itself and reaches in its effect far beyond all those deaths died for the sake of love that we find in the plays and stories of the world's literature, so that we, believing in its mystery, are at one and the same time both able to understand it and, from this understanding through faith, to draw the conclusions it implies for us. The willingness to lay down one's life for one's fellowmen is not a humanistic ideal dealt out to mankind in small doses. It keeps on the horizon of its vision the death of Christ (and therefore of the believer) and always looks back from this to man's actual situation in life. If I, fully believing, comprehend Christ's death as a death died for me, I acquire thereby (and not otherwise!) the right to view my own life as a response to this. On the reverse side, this right carries with it the duty of taking the question of death seriously, as something by means of which I interpret my own situation as a Christian.

3. *The Loneliness of Death and the Mission*

Man dies alone. Whereas life always says togetherness—even in the mother's womb—so much so that
an individual person can neither come into being
alone, nor endure, nor even be thought. Death man-
ages to suspend this law of community for an a-
temporal moment. The living can accompany the
dying to the very gates of death, and the dying can
have the feeling that they are being accompanied,
especially if the communion of the saints accompa-
nies them in their belief in Christ. In spite of this,
however, they pass through the gates of death alone.
This loneliness makes death what it now is: the consequence of sin (Rom 5:12). It is idle to speculate
what it otherwise could have been.

Christ took this death in all its finality upon himself to redeem sinners, and the dramatic power of his
action emphatically demanded not only that he
should be forsaken by all men and that he should
even dismiss the few who stood by him, but also that
he should surrender the Holy Spirit, the eternal bond
of communion that connected him to his heavenly
Father, into this Father's hands, so that the experience of being wholly forsaken even by his Father
might be endured to its limit. Love in all its diversity
and multiplicity must be simplified and reduced to its
essentials in this one unifying point, so that in

streaming out from this point it may have an eternal supply from which to spring.

For this reason there is no togetherness in faith on earth that could not have come from the ultimate loneliness of the death on the Cross. The baptismal rite, by which the Christian is immersed in water and which bears a strong symbolic likeness to the threat of death, cuts him off from every other kind of communication in order to bring him to the source where true communion begins. Consequently, faith itself must necessarily stand face to face with Christ's abandonment by God and the world. It must do so of necessity, however intensely or vaguely this sense of loneliness is experienced by the incipient believer. It is an experience of loneliness that goes beyond all earthly ties, whether physical or spiritual, a loneliness that assumes and elevates the Plotinian *monos pros monon* (the alone to the alone); the aloneness is now not God's (who is triune) but the Son's, forsaken by the Father in the giving up of the Spirit on the Cross.

Therefore, in spite of all the ridicule of modern humanistic theologians, the Christian as an isolated being really does exist. He does not need to be conceived in the way that Luther or Kierkegaard imagined him, where this individual has some difficulty understanding himself as a member of the community of saints. The biblical concept of him is sufficient for us to understand his position. Abraham arrives at belief in total loneliness, first in his confrontation

with Sarah and again with Isaac. Moses has to appear
alone before the invisible God in the burning bush,
and again, for a space of forty days, before the cloud
of glory on the mountain. Elijah meets him, but only
after longing for death and wandering for forty days
to Mount Horeb in order to say to him: "I, even I
only, am left; and they seek my life, to take it away"
(1 Kings 19:4, 10, 14). The great prophets of the
Scriptures receive their sense of mission when they
stand alone before God and while they are in a
visionary state that interrupts all communication
between them and the world. The mother of the
Lord is chosen in terrifying loneliness in order that
once she has come to understand her infinitely isolat-
ing fate, she becomes united again with mankind
through the reference to Elizabeth. Again, it is in
complete isolation, at the moment when God's light
makes him blind to everything else, that Paul
receives his calling. Nothing has ever borne fruit in
the Church without emerging from the darkness of a
long period of loneliness into the light of the community.

The objection could be raised that in all these cases
it is not so much a question of faith as a special sense
of mission. But the sense of mission manifested in the
lives of these figures is of necessity an exemplary one,
since the "pillars of the Church" determine the style
of her whole structure and provide the canonical
yardsticks for every believer. These figures serve a

mediating purpose in clarifying the position between the loneliness of Christ's mission and the faith on which the belief of every Christian is based. The sense of mission, whether great or small, which every Christian possesses, originates from the same point. It is something that, like the gifts of grace, is not distributed from within the community, but is given to "each according to the measure of faith that God has assigned him". It enters the ecclesiastical body of many members from the individual's personal encounter with God (Rom 12:3–4).

Only as an individual can a Christian be called to the service of the Church, and as a member of the Church be called to the service of the world. As an individual who stands alone, he cannot at the moment of his call be protected by any human agency. No one can take over the responsibility that he accepts when he responds affirmatively to God's call, and no one can relieve him of the burden God may subsequently place on his shoulders. No matter to what extent God may eventually bring those together who have a sense of mission, each must have first stood alone and isolated before God. And no one can receive a mission until he has unconditionally and of his own free will placed his whole life in God's hands, in the same way as a dying man, with no freedom of choice, is forced to do. Only when everything has been offered and sacrificed, only when God is free to demand what he wants without any reservations on the part of the believer, can the possibility of a Christian sense of mission arise. For only from this meeting point with the dying God can a life based on belief bear fruit. This fruit is the fruit of love, but it derives from man's willingness to sacrifice himself. Therefore it is *impossible* to bring the *love of neighbor*, as man understands this naturally, *as a condition* along with him in his one encounter with the Cross. Such an experience allows no such conditions concerning our fellowmen. The Christian love of one's neighbor is rather the result or outcome of self-sacrifice, just as God the Father made the redemption of mankind the outcome of his forsaken Son's self-sacrifice. "Unless a grain of wheat falls into the earth and dies, it remains alone; but if it dies [alone], it bears much fruit" (Jn 12:24).

And since this "much fruit" in no way accords with biological or psychological-propaganda laws but is given once and for all, the man who has died in baptism and has been resurrected by the power of God is the fruit of eternal life made manifest in temporal life. The early Church was well aware of this when she ascribed to her martyrs the power of a supernatural fertility for Christendom and the world at large. It is therefore by no means true that only a few very radically-minded Christians need to base their faith on the death of Christ, while the majority may remain content to let just a little of the transfiguring supernatural light illuminate their natural lives. That is a kind of dualism that could be better described by the use of such terms as "detachment from the world" and "openness to the world" or by considering the difference between the practice and the abstractions of the law and the commandments. For Christians there is no question of such an attitude, for "all of us who have been baptized into Jesus Christ were baptized into his death" and "we were buried therefore with him by baptism." It holds good for all Christians that "our old self was crucified with him" and that "if we have died with Christ" (Rom 6:3, 4, 6, 8) and are "buried" (Col 2:12) we are also "raised" with him and "sit with him in the heavenly places" (Eph 2:6; Col 2:12) so that "our commonwealth is in heaven" (Phil 3:2; Heb 12:22) and consequently we are "strangers and exiles on the earth" (1 Pet 2:11; Heb 11:9, 13). Mark stresses that Jesus "called to him the multitude with his disciples" when he said to them: "If any man would come after me, let him deny himself and take up his cross and follow me" (Mk 8:34ff.), and Luke does likewise (Lk 14:25ff.), adding the speech concerning the complete surrender of all earthly goods: "So therefore, whoever of you does not renounce all that he has cannot be my disciple" (Lk 14:33).

What is said up to this point is meant to apply to all Christians. Only later are distinctions made that determine the nature of the individual mission. It is all part of the disciples' attempt to follow Christ by giving up their lives out of love for the world and in obedience to God who so loved the world that he gave his only Son that the world might be saved through him. It is, therefore, when seen from the inside (and how much can already be seen from the outside?) the affirmation of earthly life in its highest form, because it is the form introduced by God himself. Man is capable of misusing and abusing everything for his own selfish ends, even the invitation to sacrifice his life for the sake of that love from which faith springs. He can interpret it as a refuge from the attacks of a hostile fate, even as a kind of insurance that guarantees him eternal life. And yet how can that moment of death and abandonment by God, when the heavens grow dark, the earth trembles and the graves open, offer a place of refuge? Does it not rather expose us in all our nakedness and frailty to the combined powers of the temporal world? There is an old prayer that contains the words: "Let me hide myself in thy wounds." But where is man more exposed than there? Where is he certain to receive more blows than there? And nevertheless man is hidden there, because it is the ultimate "placeless" place, the complete openness in death—as love.

The world possesses no other archetype of perfect love apart from this one, which was decreed and granted to it by God. It has become impossible for us to adopt as a provisional standard the humanistic self-engendering conception of love, only to accommo-

date ourselves, when this finally fails, to the love
manifested in Christ. If the one cannot be incorporated into the other and has not already received its
impress, either directly or indirectly, we shall hardly
be able to delude ourselves at the moment of failure
into believing that we have hitherto lived our lives in
love. This holds good for the Christian just as much
as for the non-Christian. By his baptism and by his
belief, the Christian is placed within the only form of
love acceptable to God, the form that proceeds
directly or indirectly from the *Ernstfall* [decisive
moment].

As Luther so rightly realized, the Christian strives
for and attains his freedom in his confrontation with
death, with Christ's death for him as an individual.
And the only valid response I can make to this is to
be prepared to die for him, and even more, to be
dead in him. The Son attained freedom by reaching
his ultimate destination (*eis telos*: Jn 13:1) and "loving
to the end", where no power could harm him, simply because all the harm that could be done him had
been done already. He remains above and beyond
everything and therefore free. *Ama sicut Christus et fac
quod vis* [love as Christ did and do what you will]—
that is, if you are still capable of action. But all of
Christ's actions in his earthly life issued from this
principle. The boldness, almost presumptuousness, of
his actions were debited to the bill of his suffering,
which had to be paid in full. His deeds are covered

by the *Ernstfall* of the Cross. By the power of the
Holy Spirit he is certain of his obedience to the very
last and therefore has command of it in advance of
his death. This is what makes him so immeasurably
superior, so absolutely authoritative in his calling. He
does not need to bind himself by any law other than
that of his own making, by the identity of his obedience and his freedom at the ultimate point of the
goal toward which he is traveling and which he will
without fail realize, because his whole life is justified
and substantiated by this initial course: "I have a baptism to be baptized with; and how I am constrained
until it is accomplished!" (Lk 12:50).

4. *The* Ernstfall *as the Origin of the Church*

The Church has her origins in the crucifixion. The
fear and agony of death, suffered in full conscious-
ness of the sin of the world and the absence of God
the Father, tear open the entrance to a realm in
which the Church can be established. Could she
have come into being without the aid of the second
Eve, whose willing acceptance of God's command
first opened up the way for the incarnation of his
Son and was then remembered at the moment of the
Son's death-agony, demanding assent to this also?
Our faith tells us that the answer is no. We are
unable to penetrate to the mystery of this twofold

fruitfulness ("Woman, behold your son!"). The assent of the Son in death stands in the space of the Father's denial; the assent of his mother to the death of her Son stands in the space of His denial. She is left standing alone, even sent away in order to become more united to Him who has been left alone and sent away by the Father. Christ's assent is the assent of a man, inasmuch as he takes upon himself the guilt and the God-forsakenness of all men. Mary's assent is that of a woman, inasmuch as she consents to her Son's suffering and total submission in the darkness of death. She can help in no other way than by letting it happen, with the full knowledge of who her Son really is. The swords that pierce her heart seem from our human standpoint more cruel than the nails that pierce her Son's hands and feet, since her experience of God's love depends on her first consenting from the depths of her heart, and without any protest, to the very worst that befalls not herself, but her Son. For it is as if she were doing what the mother and bride would most fear doing and seek by all means to avoid—that is, herself piercing the body and spirit of her Son like a sword. "Suffer! Die! Experience the very worst that it is possible to experience!" It is as if the mother, with the deepest imaginable love, were obliged to wield the weapons that sinners had turned against her Son in their hatred of him. And it is as if the Son willingly let it happen, in order that his mother might be initiated into the ultimate mystery of his death as into the ultimate horror of the death-dealing world.

This fearful need for love to give its assent to death, this "unbloody martyrdom" on the part of Mary, is the crucial situation out of which the Church springs to life. It is the fertility of the Mater Dolorosa, the apocalyptic woman in her birth pangs. The cry uttered by the Church at her birth is heard at the same moment as the mother's inaudible cry uttered as she beholds her dying Son. This death cry is, however, only the final outcome of that original assent given in Nazareth, which accorded God the freedom to carry out a divine plan unforeseeable in its consequences and reaching far beyond the powers of man. Mary's original assent already carried within it the seeds of death, whether she was aware of it or not. It was an assent to which no limits could be set (for who would presume to prescribe limits to God's power?) and which therefore contained within itself the willing assent to death and to being killed, since it is "according to thy Word".

This assent is the source and origin of all prayer. Prayer receives its standard in this assent: to the extent this assent reaches the Father, to that extent a word is a prayer. First of all comes the invitation of the angel opening up the realm in which our assent may be received. These words of assent then fulfill the promises they express on the cross, where they

become flesh that is sacrificed and consumed, so that
the original assent may be seen to have been pure and
complete. All of Mary's prayers and supplications to
the Son and all of the Son's prayers and supplications
to the Father take place within the realm of an abiding assent to the will of the Father. All thanks offered
in prayer are a radiation of that unconditional willingness to receive grace in the ways decreed by the
Father. No prayer can make conditions. We can be
said to pray in earnest only when we decide to offer
ourselves unconditionally to God, however timid we
may feel. Under the law of the old covenant and
before the appearance of Mary, it was still possible to
bargain and haggle with God, because his Word had
not descended from heaven to be crucified, and man
in his suffering seemed as a result to have a certain
superiority over God. But since the crucifixion this is
no longer possible, because the unconditional consent
of Mary, together with the boundless obedience of
the Son, has become the core and essence of the
Church. From this moment onward her nature and
mode of prayer and approach to God are fixed and
determined. They have become the "law, according
to which you entered with your inheritance; and neither time, nor any temporal power shall prevail
against that which has developed into fullness as a living form".

In order that this law, laid down in the first hour
of the Church's history, should be not just a memory

receding farther and farther into the past as century
follows century but should rather remain the origin
of what is forever present and living, the mystery of
the Eucharist has been made the basis and foundation
of the Church. In the Eucharist the hour of the
Church's birth remains a permanently present reality,
coinciding with the hour of Christ's death. The
Church celebrates her birth not as something that
already exists, but as something that is in the process
of happening in each offering of the Mass, in each
Communion; and this in the event of the death of
the Lord: "For as often as you eat this bread and
drink the cup, you proclaim the Lord's death until he
comes" (1 Cor 11:26). Catherine of Siena's concept
of the Church originates in this idea of the constantly
repeated and renewed act of making Christ's blood
flow from the cross—an act that on each and every
occasion brings with it reatonement, resanctification
and reunion of the bride and the groom at the bridegroom's death. And Catherine is simply the highest
and most self-reliant exponent of the eucharistic
piety that we find expressed in those descriptions of
the Mass as a "mystical winepress" or a vine, or in
the reverence paid to pictures of bleeding wafers and
the bleeding Heart of the Lord, or in the cult and
presentation of the "Church emanating from the
wound in his side", which is at the same time the
Church catching Christ's blood in the cup of suffering, and so on. We may reject these illustrations of

the eucharistic mystery as being too primitive or melodramatic for our own taste and age. But this makes it all the more incumbent for us to give more serious consideration to the mystery, "the living form developed to perfection", which all these illustrations attempt to express. It is the form from which the Church originated, so that all the belief of the Church in Christ can be a belief directed only toward this form.

In fact, if Mary's faith as the maternal-bridal *ecclesia* comes from this event, so is the faith of Peter, the visible, male-hierarchical Church, essentially ordered to this. The Church of Peter has her being in Peter's confession of faith, in a belief that transcends "flesh and blood" and is established by the Father in heaven. Overriding the subjective elements in Peter's faith, Christ takes advantage of the objective element it contains to make it the rock on which he builds his Church and to bind his disciple to fulfilling a future obligation, which God will offer him as his ultimate fate (*eschaton*): " 'Truly, truly, I say to you . . . when you are old, you will stretch out your hands, and another will gird you and carry you where you do not wish to go.' This he said to show by what death he was to glorify God" (Jn 21:18–19). Even Peter—unwillingly, but allowing the will of another to prevail—will eventually arrive at that point in life at which Mary stood, while he stood apart and denied and wept.

Between the opposing situations represented by Mary and Peter, the fixed but living form of the Church undergoes development, and she cannot escape from this course. At every moment in the present she is concerned with arriving at the future, where she regains her unrealized origins. For who in the Church could ever claim to be standing where Mary once stood? For the Church, the future is the arrival of that moment of the "sign of the Son of Man coming with the clouds" and of the eyes of man as an existential being opened to behold it. *Videbunt in quem transfixerunt:* "They shall be free to look on him whom they have pierced" (cf. Zech 12:10 = Jn 19:37 = Rev 1:7).

The Church in her truth is determined by the form of her origin and her end. What happens between these points is insofar Church (as "Body" and "Bride") as she relates it to this form: "My children with whom I am in labor again until Christ is formed in you" (Gal 4:19), and we must assume "the emptied form of servant" in order to be "of the mind of Jesus Christ" (cf. Phil 2:5–6). This holds true because the Church is not an abstract collective or a "moral subject", but the profoundly mysterious reality of a second Eve formed for a second Adam—as concrete and personal a figure as he himself, and therefore existing as an extension of the original, personal, canonical attitude, only in a vast number of different persons who become part of her through

christological grace. The Church is an edifice supported by "pillars" (Rev. 3:12; Gal 2:9). She is "built
upon the foundation of the apostles and prophets,
Jesus Christ himself being the cornerstone, in whom
the whole structure is joined together and grows into
a holy temple in the Lord" (Eph 2:20–21). This ontological structure is eternally fixed and revealed in the
perfected vision of the heavenly Jerusalem, which was
bequeathed to the twelve disciples as a foundation for
the apostolic Church and which, moreover, derives
from the social structure of Israel as a nation consist-
ing of twelve tribes.

The God of Israel was first of all the God of Abraham, and it was through Abraham that the pregnant
form of God's promise to man was first imprinted on
man's completely open faith. The God who made
this promise was the God of Abraham, Isaac and
Jacob, indicating the linear nature with its threefold
stress underlying the personal foundation of the
Hebrew nation as a whole and corresponding to the
mysterious appearance of God as three Persons by
the oaks of Mamre (cf. Gen 18:1). After that (and not
before) come the twelve sons and from these the
twelve tribes. This form, developed to completion
under the new covenant, is no longer of a linear and
chronological nature, but rather of the nature of a cli-
max in time, as in the sense of a wedding, at which
the assent on the cross represents the coming union
of bride and bridegroom (cf. Rev. 19:7, 9). From this

ring of fulfillment the twelve are sent, but to each of the twelve belongs another twelve (the character of the founder is handed on to the Church by means of the apostles) before the thousands "from all tribes and tongues, people and nations," unite themselves behind this hundred and forty-four.

The twelve who come after the disciples, and themselves act in their capacity as individuals in bringing the Church to the people, are undoubtedly those believers who have accepted Christ's way of life (which is at the same time Mary's) as their own and have based their existence solely on their willing assent to obey the commands of the Father, being actively prepared for such obedience, first by renouncing their earthly goods and living in poverty, and second by renouncing any close human ties and living in chastity. This christological-mariological way of life has as its most pregnant form the love-death that took place both on the cross and beside it. In the face of death everyone is, of course, reduced of necessity to obedience, poverty and chastity. However, the chosen twelve (or whatever the number may be who base their lives on those of the founders and pillars of the Church) willingly accept this way of life in advance—a way of life that contains hidden within itself this power to redeem the world by means of Christ's action and grace. For since he was obedient to the point of death, God gave him the lordly name of redeemer of the world (cf. Phil 2:8–11); since he accepted poverty as his lot, he can make all others rich (2 Cor 8:11, 6:10); since he chose chastity he can wed himself to the whole Church as his bride (2 Cor 11:2), and thus fulfill eucharistically the mysteries of paradise and of the Song of Solomon concerning the flesh (cf. Eph 5:27): "The body is not meant for immorality, but for the Lord, and the Lord for the body" (1 Cor 6:13). The meaningful sharing of the life of Christ and Mary within the Church cannot be reserved for any particular group of eccentrics who stand, as it were, in some side chapel of the high altar and celebrate their particular Mass apart from the main body of worshipers. If the sharing is to be meaningful, it must take place at the meeting point in the Church between her founders and pillars and the broad stream of worshipers, or at the point where the Church begins to rise from her foundations and grow into an edifice; at no time, however, can this edifice detach itself from its foundations or develop into an independent structure. The Church is rather "God's building", created by "God's fellow workers" (1 Cor 3:9) upon her foundation stone, out of which she may therefore be said to grow (*auxei:* Eph 2:21) as a series of single stones, all of which willingly allow themselves to be "like living stones . . . built into a spiritual house" (1 Pet 2:5). The result of this willingness is that the single stones take on something of the character of the pillars of the Church and themselves become a "holy priesthood" offering "spiritual sacrifices" (ibid.)—that is, presenting their bodies as a living sacrifice (cf. Rom 12:1). In so doing, they have in their spiritual temper a share of the life of those who teach the message of Christ (cf. 1 Cor 7:29–31).

The married state (and the state of being a possessor and disposer of worldly goods, which goes with it) is in itself a state of God's earthly creation and therefore subject to the ravages of time. It becomes a state of Christian witness according to the degree to which the spirit of the Christ–Mary state can be realized within it—that is, as an integral part of it and not in a way that would stunt its growth (cf. 1 Cor 7:2–5). It is brought about by the twofold action of the sacrament of marriage and the attitude of mind of the married partners. The blessing given to such a union comes directly from the Cross, and the grace obtained thereby is mediated from the borderline between life and death. This grace has the nature of a self-renouncing love: husband and wife offer up to each other their rule over their own bodies (1 Cor 7:4); the wife becomes the husband's "own flesh", and his self-love becomes love for her (Eph 5:28). The rule and the norm for both partners are represented by the chaste exchange of bodies between Christ and his Church.

It was necessary to mention this here in order to make it quite clear that the Church can be described morphologically only when she is at the same time seen from a genetic point of view. Only her growth and development out of the *morphe* of Christ can explain her nature and being. She has no being when detached from Christ, because she is a constant development out of him, and the point from which she develops is always the point at which the miraculous exchange "between sin and grace, death and life," takes place, namely, on the Cross. Only on the Cross does the significance of God's Incarnation become manifest. It is therefore impossible to speak of a "tendency toward incarnation" on the part of God, as a development taking place in world history, without first accepting the purpose of this development. Even the condition of the Church as a condition of immanent development (as, for example, of a "holy people") cannot be understood unless one continually bears in mind out of whose person she develops and to whose law she is subject. If she is the tree that grew out of the "grain of mustard seed" of the Cross, then she is also the tree that will herself bear the same seed and, as a result, repeat the pattern of the crucifixion. In bearing this seed the Church returns to the point of her origin.

5. *The Mystery of Glory*

The Cross is the self-glorification of the love of God in the world. This can be understood only if one takes into consideration and fully believes in its hidden meaning, which is that in taking upon itself all the sins of the world—in being plunged into the darkest of nights—eternal love surrenders itself to the uttermost limits of God-forsakenness in order to prove itself, at the moment of its greatest weakness, stronger than all the guilt and sin of the world. Not only physical death, but also the experience that it is the outcome of sin, is suffered in such a way that it becomes a proclamation of eternal love and consequently of eternal life. The complete surrender of free will in the experience of suffering (the nailing of the body to the cross corresponds to the ever more terrifying bondage of the spirit) remains an expression of the highest kind of free will: "For this reason the Father loves me, because I lay down my life that I may take it again. No one takes it from me, but I lay it down of my own accord. I have power to lay it down, and I have power to take it again" (Jn 10:17–18).

The power to regain life completely is contained in the capacity for its total self-surrender. There can be absolutely no doubt as to the resurrection of the Son: death and resurrection are simply the two naturally reverse aspects of one and the same act of love. The glory that manifests itself on Easter is already present in the veiled glory of Good Friday, just as the column of God in the desert could appear dark at one moment and shining the next. For the glory is decisively the self-glorifying love of God manifested to all the world. In the final instance love is its own reward, which does not mean to say that the promise of the greatest imaginable joy could ever exclude the deepest suffering: darkness and light are correlatives in Jesus Christ's epiphany of love. But they are correlatives in the sense that the love issuing from the spear-wound in the side of the resurrected Christ streams forth into the Church and the world: the seal on God's love is broken open. With the opening-up of the heart, the Holy Spirit is freed on the one hand as the Spirit of the Father, who let his Son suffer because he so loved the world, and on the other hand as the Spirit of the Son, who resigned it to the Father before his death in order to suffer the total death of spiritual abandonment. The wounds are transfigured, the Spirit is pentecostal and the Church is bathed in the light of Easter, which the Word has earned for it. But all the transfiguration and transparency of Christian existence stream from the darkness of death; even at the crucifixion Christ ceases to be bound by the limits of finite time, just as little as he is bound by it during his descent into hell. Consequently, his action is not to be considered as belonging to the past (the reenactment of his death in the Eucharist should warn us against making this mistake). His action can be considered as belonging to the past only insofar as it is an irreversible act of redemption that takes place between the time of his crucifixion and his Resurrection. The Church is founded in and upon this act.

But this is where we have to be careful and bear in mind that the journey into that night of suffering and death is also the journey to the extreme limits of this earthly life. On this journey the human (and divine) love of our Lord measures out to the full its own final dimensions. It becomes the ideal, the totality, the highest norm of human love. "Greater love hath no man . . ." The paschal glory is the world beyond, on the threshold of which the gates of eternal life open to admit Christ as he dies in this world. He is admitted in his entirety—mind, body and soul. The new, heavenly and eucharistic Lord can no longer be considered part of the old cosmos. The dimension that opens up, in order to receive the cosmos—in the figure of "Christ the first fruits" (1 Cor 15:23)—into glory, is in no way attainable by that cosmos, not even at some distant time in the future. World history by no means represents a progressive Christianization of the cosmos, either with the aid of the Eucharist and its usefulness for worldly ends, or by the employment of "godly virtues" in the common service of mankind. Such a view of history fails to take into account two things—namely, that the sign of those "last things" (*eschaton*) in this world is Christ's death by crucifixion, and, consequently, that both the Church and the individual Christian are rooted in and sustained by the double mystery of his death and Resurrection, "becoming like him in his death, that if possible I may attain the resurrection from the dead"

(Phil 3:10–11). "And you were buried with him in baptism, in which you were also raised with him through faith in the working of God, who raised him from the dead" (Col 2:12). This turning point is vouchsafed to Christians as the very center of their existence.

Where does it place them? It places them in a position impossible to determine from the viewpoint of the world as it was before Christ's appearance. In default of a better term, one could describe it as eschatological, and Christians as eschatological beings, but this would be to misunderstand their position, for what would it mean? That they stand at a point at which, by the grace of God, the old world turns toward the new one? That they are spared the "curse" of Christ's death because "Christ redeemed us from the curse of the law, having become a curse for us" (Gal 3:13), and yet by God's grace they may "become like him in his death" (Phil 3:10), even at baptism, at the very beginning of their lives as Christians in order to have in all their earthly doings their "hearts" (Mt 6:21) and their "commonwealth" already in heaven (Phil 3:20)? When all is said and done, where can they be said to be at home? The answer is, basically, in the event that constitutes Christ's death and Resurrection, in "forgetting what lies behind and straining forward to what lies ahead" (Phil 3:12–14) and in striving earnestly to enter God's rest (Heb 4:11), like people who "thus make it clear that they are seeking a homeland" (Heb 11:14) and "run with perseverance the race that is set before them" (Heb 12:1). And this race, the Epistle to the Hebrews tells us, is to be run with Christ as our guide and our goal: "Consider him who endures from sinners such hostility against himself, so that you may not grow weary or fainthearted. In your struggle against sin you have not yet resisted to the point of shedding your blood" (Heb 12:3–4). It is therefore a race that is run within the limits set by Christ himself and judged according to the extreme standards of his struggle against the sin of the world. The Christian lives in the sphere of an event that signifies absolute love—that is, in a boundless realm beyond which nothing greater can be imagined (*id quo maius cogitari non potest*). If one tries to imagine something greater, to sail for new horizons, he falls into a void that eventually destroys the man who was created for the sake of something greater than the world we know. This is not simply an "idea" transcending absolute "being". It is expressly an event taking place in the world and constituting the essence and sum total of that "being"—the absolute triune love enacted between the Father and the Son in the Holy Spirit. It is a human and genuinely historical event because God became incarnate, and at the same time it is an event that transcends history, which comes just as immediately to me as to everyone else.

For the Christian this event forms the very center of existence, and he sees everything of any consequence in this world as gravitating toward it. There can be no question of this event of death and resurrection standing at the last end of the world and so constituting a peripheral phenomenon that one could ignore with impunity until the Christian has carried out his duties in a "worldly world". On the contrary, he sees all worldly considerations as grouping themselves concentrically around this center, which in its peculiar quality of a *mysterium* radiates its light over all existing things. For the Christian there is no "neutral" form of existence, which is not affected or illuminated by the mystery of absolute love, and whose fortuitous and doubtful nature is not justified or made meaningful by it. Everything appertaining to the world had to be of this nature, in order that the absolute love that God wished to communicate to the world could be embodied in an event taking place in the world. However profane the world may be in its actions and attitudes, it is bathed in the sacral light of absolute love, which not only illuminates it externally but penetrates its innermost recesses.

Why? Because God became flesh. Because the body in which the soul is made manifest is also of clay. Because Christianity is not a religion of "spirit and water", but of Spirit, water and blood, which, being indivisibly one, bear a common witness: "This is he who came by water and blood, Jesus Christ, not with the water only but with the water and the blood. And the Spirit is the witness, because the Spirit is the truth. There are three witnesses, the Spirit, the water and the blood; and these three agree" (1 Jn 5:6–8). Christianity will not exist for very long where it is merely inward or a thing of the mind. Paradoxically enough, the glory of God is already visible even in the Old Testament, in spite of the fact that all images were forbidden. It was already visible for the patriarchs, for Moses, for the people on Mount Sinai, for David and Solomon, and for the prophets. And whoever has once beheld this glory is then also aware of it in the whole of creation (Ps 19, 97, and so on). This paradoxical manifestation of God's glory is not only taken over by the New Testament (*kathoratai*: Rom 1:20) but is brought to completion in the "glory" of Christ. "We have beheld it" (*etheasametha*: Jn 1:14) once and for all at the moment when blood and water flowed from the side of the wounded Christ: "He who saw it (*heorakos*) has borne witness" (Jn 19:35). "God's glory making itself manifest" here means God's glory appearing within the field of vision of man as a creature composed of both spirit and flesh. It means even more: God's glory taking possession of man's field of vision in order to make itself manifest. The final manifestation of the glory that will make everything else fade before the truth of its evidence ("Behold, he is coming with the clouds, and every eye will see him": Rev 1:7; Mt 24:30) has already begun, according to the testimony of the disciples, with the existence of Jesus Christ.

In the New Testament, just as in the Old, it is a question of the manifestation of that which by its very nature cannot be beheld (Jn 1:18; 1 Tim 6:16); that which is in itself inaccessible to us reveals itself in all its glory (Titus 2:13), not so that man may gain control over it, but so that he may be admitted into the higher realm in which it has its being. Existence in the openness of this realm is what we call belief— the acceptance and affirmation in being taken possession of by God in Christ. Hidden within itself, it contains the hope of partially sharing in the eternal life of love, of which the opening-up of this realm is already an offer. To base one's existence on these three things means to live one's life on the basis of the *Ernstfall.* Only such an existence is witness (*martyrion*) to the truth from which it lives.

What has become of this witness in our day and age? In order to understand the ways in which Christians of today attempt to bear witness to this truth, it is necessary to begin by examining what the modern world offers in the way of an all-embracing concept as an alternative to Christian belief.

II

The Philosophical System
and Its Alternative

1. *The Theses of the System*

The Eastern and Western Powers, though split politically, converge in an average overall philosophy that is already nearly achieved and so lets itself be described in a preliminary fashion without any special prophetic gift. And just as today, so will they in the future possess in their mature form innumerable deviations and sects but will cover them all with one wide roof. But this comprehensiveness will at the same time be the radical background form of the system, which as such is its own *Ernstfall*. Nor will it fail to manifest itself as such in the course of time.

Even before Hegel and again after him, it was Kant, with his twofold assertion concerning the self-criticism of reason in its limitedness and the absolute (infinite) character of freedom, who created a new and decisive point of departure for philosophical speculation. In the Middle Ages the two parts of this assertion would still have been seen as contradicting each other. For, either a nature that can measure its own reason as limited somewhere shares in unlimited reason and truth so that it can possess a moment of unlimitedness in its own freedom, or the nature that explains its reason seriously as limited would have to admit the "limitedness" of its own freedom (because reason and will are only two correlative aspects of the one spirit). No so Kant. As he sees it, the act of critical self-limitation in the realm of reason becomes an assumption of power on the part of man within a limited sphere, from which—as from the surface of the tiny ball of the earth set in motion by man—the examination of the surrounding space of ideas becomes possible. The image, surprisingly enough, is Kant's own. The man who relies on the evidence of his senses sees the earth as a flat surface with a circular horizon. Experience teaches him that wherever he goes he always sees a space around him in which he could proceed farther, and thus he knows the limits of his actual knowledge of the earth at any given time, "but not the limits of all possible geography. But if I have gone so far as to know that the earth is a sphere and that its surface is spherical, I am able even from a small part of it—for instance, from the magnitude of a degree—to know determinately, in accordance with principles *a priori*, the diameter, and through it the total superficial area, of the earth. Our reason is not like a plane indefinitely far extended, the limits of which we know only in a general way, but must rather be compared to a sphere, whose radius can be determined from the curvature of the arc of its surface—that is to say, from the nature of synthetic *a priori* suppositions—whereby we can likewise specify with certainty its volume and its limits." [1]

This remarkable use of an image drawn from science and applied to spiritual reality gives us—no

[1] Immanuel Kant, *Critique of Pure Reason*, trans. Norman Kemp (London, 1929).

matter what interpretations Kant and his followers may give of it—the key to the main problem: Infinity (or freedom) is the means of measuring our own finite nature; with it man measures his own diameter. If this means is previously given him (in nature), he is able, to the extent that he grasps it (in spirit), to take possession of it and steer himself. His autonomy proves itself precisely in this possession of his diameter. Later on, Schelling stresses even more emphatically the indeterminacy of human freedom (but also its equal infinity with God), and Sartre takes its finite nature for granted, as a precondition of it. Thus, what was originally maintained on a purely speculative basis in the realm of German idealistic philosophy became subsequently corroborated on an empirical basis by man's experimental attempts to control his own destiny: Essence becomes (cybernetically, pharmaceutically, or whatever) the function of existence freely outlining itself.

The second thesis to be maintained is substantially in agreement with the first. As Fichte shows, freedom exists speculatively only as an intrasubjective phenomenon, as a free community within the community. It takes the form of a dialogue in which the "thou" interrogates and is in its turn interrogated. Feuerbach sees "the divine" manifesting itself among men within this dialogical realm, and Marx draws the practical conclusions of Feuerbach's observations by insisting on the induction and development of this realm, at whatever cost and by whatever means, because it is there that the principle of intrasubjectivity can unfold on a totally human scale. Every creature who has a share in the uniquely precious essence of autonomy and emerges from nature into the realm of freedom belongs, as an inhabitant of this dialogical spirit-world, to the realm of the absolute and has a claim to the protection afforded by the rights of man. This is the ethic of humanism.

The third thesis is the decisive one. The cosmos cannot from this point be any longer considered speculatively other than as the self-mediation of freedom (Fichte, Schelling, Hegel). If this freedom represents the absolute, though in finite form, it must gain possession of itself through nature or the non-ego by overcoming the limits of objectivity and developing from an idea into a reality. What was thought out on a purely speculative basis in idealistic philosophy has been corroborated in the most remarkable way by the empirical theory of evolution: that nature is an *évolution créatrice*; that it develops its forms one out of the other in mounting succession with the aid of an upthrusting dynamism. But whose dynamism? That of the spirit, no doubt, that longs to return to itself and—as an idea on which the whole of the natural realm is founded—strives toward itself as freedom in its realized state. The natural realm becomes the mine that yields the material for a process of hominization. With Fichte it was only speculative, but since

Marx it has become practical and increasingly technical. And because man is seen as the center and aim of
this process, nature itself loses its aura of a mediating
agency for the divine purpose and is reduced to
being a "worldly world".

The fourth thesis emerges as a corollary to the
others. As the circle between the ideal and the real
gradually closes, all being is seen as contained within
it, so that a God who stood outside this circle would
be superfluous, unless one were to consider the
establishment of human freedom a divine occur-
rence. The spirit is by definition absolute and lord
over itself. It is therefore possible to do as Hegel
does and include all forms of religion, as preliminary
stages of absolute knowledge, within this circle. It is
possible, if they really are stages that man, as an isolated spirit and still bound by the laws of nature and
his symbolizing mind, can look up to (or down at)
in awe and respect as the ideal of his own
fulfillment. But the absolute cannot be doubled. The
moment may possibly arrive when the names attrib-
uted to the system—such as theism (pantheism) and
atheism—are no longer felt to be of a different
value. Fichte was able to defend himself against the
charge of being an atheist out of the deepest religious conviction, and Hegel would have similarly
refused to tolerate the use of such an epithet with
regard to himself. Those of Hegel's followers who
stand on the left, however, accept the inference of

atheism as a matter of course and hardly consider it worthy of discussion.

At this particular moment, we are not concerned with the naming of the system. What really concerns us is the unbalancing power of that impetus (or weight of inertia!) that was able to produce the fourth thesis out of the first three. We may say without doubt that if the cosmos does indeed represent a process of hominization, and if the aim of this process (human freedom) is by definition an absolute one (i.e., autonomous), then it must necessarily follow that the *causa finalis* of evolution is at the same time its *causa efficiens* and also its *primum movens*. The existence of the cosmos is explained by its aim— man. But the freedom of man (dialogically interpreted as love) is self-creating and requires no aid outside itself. With this explanation all proofs of God's existence—cosmological or otherwise—are found to be invalid and removed from even the "contingent" position to which they had already been relegated. The triumph of the system resides in the fact that what began as an attempt at a speculative supposition was later corroborated on an empirical basis, with the consequence that it can now be manipulated with impunity in a purely experimental way.

2. *The Implications of the System*

The system has its roots in the ground of speculation, but it lifts its trunk and branches into the air of exact science and no longer requires the aid of speculation except to provide an occasional hypothesis for experiments. But the comparison used by Kant reveals that even the speculative method was influenced and directed by images drawn from natural science. Kant wrote a theoretical philosophy that was to make possible the strict scientific method required for the study of natural science. He based his philosophy on the distinction between matter (perception) and form (concept) and presented it in such a way as to show that the material world could be controlled by the intellect. Ever since Descartes, Bacon and Hobbes, all philosophical thought has been an attempt at some kind of control. "Facts" had to be brought under certain "laws". The facts were there, and it seemed idle to inquire into their origins. Later on, speculative philosophy was to explain them as being derived from the spirit. The doubt as to whether they really existed and the disquiet that this doubt caused were stilled by the consoling idea of the absolute nature of the spirit, which embraces the factual world and is not open to any such questioning doubt. But earlier, Leibnitz had already postulated the existence of the most perfect essences as originating and developing out of their own structure, and in this way he explained the ontological argument for the existence of God in this best of all possible worlds. As a result, the truly basic difference between essence and existence disappears as far as this best of all possible worlds is concerned (best or not, it is the *only* possible world). And neither idealistic philosophy nor the systems that follow it are able to recover this difference, because the distinction presupposes at the origin of the world a free creator (and not an idea postulating itself as existing). Not even in the form given by Heidegger can the distinction be reintroduced into the system, because it cannot be exploited in any scientific or technical way.

Whereas metaphysics in its medieval form was constructed on a double axis—

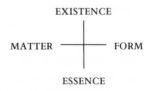

—the metaphysics of the system is reduced to the horizontal axis. The vertical axis derives originally from the awe and wonder experienced by philosophers at the incomprehensible, inexplicable and sovereign nature of reality (*energeia, actualitas*) as it concerns both man and nature, and from the gaping distinction between the surplus of being that can never be attained and exhausted by the sum of all existent beings. "How can nothingness enter into being?" asks Plato in his *Theaitetos*. Or how is it possible to have a finite or transitory share in what is presupposed as a fullness of being? This awe and wonder, which is scientifically unfruitful because it cannot be exploited, is therefore dropped in the systematic investigations of later philosophers. Philosophy is reduced to a doctrine of the spirit (in which spirit develops through matter) and, as a final consequence, to anthropology. For man becomes the all-embracing idea, and it is idle to think of him as measurable or embraced by being unless one relates this being to the spiritual and creative God who remains an alien body and does not fit into the system.

Man has his place in the midst of the system, of which he is its perfection, but only so as to know it, and not so that he would be able repeatedly (asymptotically, Fichte says) to reach and conquer it. Hegel, as essentially a theoretical philosopher, assumes a position nearer to the completion of this process, while Marx, as a practical man and a prophet, assumes a midway position, at a point where the process is about to erupt into the realm of freedom. In any case, what is to become of man himself—who is seen as the ultimate goal of this process—is a paradoxical matter. For Hegel has sacrificed him as an individual to the idea in its realized state, and Marx has continually sacrificed him to an idea that has to be realized. The system demands that this contradiction be accepted, because there can be no question of immortality or resurrection. Man as an individual, in order to retain his autonomy, is obliged to renounce every hope of fulfilling his existence other than through this idea of totality. The dialogical encounter, the ordering of man and wife, and so on, may possibly evoke this idea, but it cannot fill it out. Anthropology as a totality can lead only to the total sacrifice of man—in favor of "humanity", which, after all, consists of nothing but men. The ethic of anthropology is a kind of altruism, demanding an absolute love for the All (God as a realized idea) as for any fellow creature, and a willingness on the part of the individual to blot himself out and perish in the interests of the fellow creature who represents this idea.

3. *The Alternative to the System*

Compared with the many times fragmented thought of late antiquity, which in many respects was beginning to crumble when the early Christians arrived with their message of salvation, the thought of the system we are discussing is closed and is becoming more and more self-contained. How a Christian of today is to confront a world that subscribes to such a system is a question of the greatest seriousness.

The most obvious answer would seem to be that he should make the system his own and at the same time be critical of it: "Examine it thoroughly and retain what is good in it." In this case he should try to retrace from a Christian viewpoint the development of philosophical thought in the modern era and, by starting again from precisely those points at which Kant, Fichte and Hegel had their greatest influence, attempt to redirect the current of thought. Almost the whole of present-day scholarship is concerned with doing just that. After a Christian Schelling (condemned in the person of Guenther, but reappearing again and again, especially in the great and convincing figure of Soloviev) there comes a Christian Hegel, first of all among the French. Then comes a Christian Fichte, who is just beginning to be accepted as the actual Church Father of modern Scholasticism since Maréchal. But this is all mere imitation of an inferior kind. The epoch-making changes in thought brought about by Hegel and Marx have had their effect, and they cannot be reversed. By detaching philosophy from its speculative beginnings, these changes have produced their own type of human being and molded him in such a way that he has accepted the idea of intellectually controlling his own destiny, as if it were second nature to him, and has adjusted himself without a murmur to the paradoxical ethic described above.

The situation in which the present-day Christian finds himself is irreversible insofar as he is viewed by the world of systematic philosophy as something that belongs purely to the past—indeed, to a past that was above all a precondition of this system and from which it therefore cannot escape because it is necessarily built into its foundations. When, for instance, one examines the main theses of the present system, must one not admit that Christianity itself made the development of the three most important ones possible? Is not the idea of freedom, unknown to the world of antiquity, an outcome of the biblical view, in which the living God first asks man to decide for or against him (the old covenant) and finally gives man a share in the supernatural freedom of the Spirit by sending his Son into the world? Furthermore, has not the Christian idea of freedom found expression in the doctrine—undoubtedly inspired by Christianity—of the worth of the individual human being and the rights of man in general? Finally, does not the idea of elevating man above the cosmos and enabling him to understand its growth and development as centered on himself have its first foundation in the biblical account of creation, in which man is seen as ruler over the whole realm of nature? Was it not necessary that these three fundamentally Christian notions should eventually be taken out of the hands of the Church (which apparently did not know what to do with them) and be entrusted to speculative philosophy on the one hand, and to the French Revolution and Marxism on the other, where they could be properly developed? Why oppose such an obviously logical development by refusing to deduce the fourth thesis from the first three and pay the tribute demanded by the rise of the secular spirit? It would at least be a retirement with full honors. It would be a "withdrawal" in the Hegelian sense of a preliminary stage being incorporated and preserved in a succeeding and higher stage, though at the cost of its own independence. It would become a "movement toward", which is the only possibility of survival the system offers.

The Christian is obviously faced with making a very difficult decision. If we assume that he is opposed to being made a part of this process and wants to preserve his Christianity intact, how is he to set about it and what form will his actions take? There is the purely practical problem of how he, as a man with a message, is to speak to and find common ground with his fellow man, who is already dyed in the wool of the system. Then there is the more serious problem of how far he should go in the course of solidarity with his fellow man in adopting the perspectives of the system. The most serious problem of all is one that concerns his conscience: As a "modern" man, how can he be a Christian? Or should he refuse to be modern and up to date, for the sake of Christ? If he does the latter, he runs the risk of being ignored by everyone and falling prey to a kind of schizophrenia by trying to live in two different centuries at once. In any case, does not Christ expressly state that we should learn to read and understand the signs of the times?

Then, it is clear that he must bestir himself and go in search of his brother. In one sense he is always with him, because he is himself a child of his time. In another sense he is sent by Christ and is not a free man; he has a message to deliver and must do it in such a way that he can be understood. He must even try to find some common ground between his own view of the world and that of his fellow men—as a kind of solidarity. He must attempt to bridge the gulf that lies between Christ and our own times. Therefore, he cannot avoid reading the Gospels and examining the development of the Church from a modern and historically enlightened point of view. He cannot do so without trying out a few experiments and hypotheses and trusting to them at least a little of the way. But it will also presumably be necessary for him to put aside the problem of the *Ernstfall* of Christ's death and Resurrection and the question of our willingness to follow him along the path of self-sacrifice, at least until these great transpositions, which have shown themselves to be unavoidable, have been attempted and sufficiently carried through. The Christian must be given time to survey the situation and think about it if he is to fulfill his Christian duty and speak and act in a way that will be intelligible to the world of today. Just at present, at the point where he has to make his decision in favor of the *Ernstfall*, there hangs a placard that says: "Road temporarily closed for repairs."

We want, in what follows, to pursue this Christian on his way—ways that today are well traveled highways. We would like to know whither they lead him. But if we were told that they would not lead us back so quickly to the Christian *Ernstfall* unless the closed part of the road were made viable in the foreseeable future, we simply would not have time to wait so long in our short lives. We would prefer to abide by our convictions—"For I know whom I have believed" (2 Tim 1:12)—to judge the system accordingly, and possibly even let it founder. Perhaps a decision based on faith would enable us to distinguish much more easily between the quality of the different spirits—that of the system and that of Christianity—because in the latter case all is measured according to the evidence manifested to us by Christ of an inexhaustible love (*id quo maius cogitari non potest*).

The whole question of a possible alternative to the system is, therefore, not so much a matter of choosing between a conservative or a progressive attitude, as of discovering whether it is possible for a Christian to ignore or put aside the challenge of the *Ernstfall* to follow Christ's example for the sake of an *aggiornamento*. In other words: *Is it possible for him to make intellectual experiments concerning his faith unless his capacity for loving is fully engaged in this activity?* For, as we have seen, the object of our faith is none other than the manifestation on the Cross of God's inexhaustible love for all men and for me as an individual.

The aim in these few pages is not, of course, an attempt at a "refutation" of the "system". That is only of indirect concern. However, it is not so difficult to see that the kind of freedom attainable only by an impersonal force cannot be called absolute freedom and that, furthermore, no idea can transpose itself into the order of reality (unless into a realm of thought totally oblivious of being) without the aid of a God, free and fully existent since eternity, to accompany it at every stage in its process of realization. The whole progress of the world points to there being a creator whose purpose is to bring about, by means of his creative powers, a free response from his creatures below, so that they may move toward him and finally be united with him in a marriage of love.

III

The Suspension of the Decisive Moment

And what, Father, is the connection
between this teaching and that of the Gospel?

Pascal, *Provincial Letters*

1. Halving the Mystery

Kant respects the empirical basis of natural science and sees that our knowledge does not reach beyond what is verifiable by the senses. This knowledge is arrived at by an interaction between man's sense perceptions and his intellect and is therefore anthropological and anthropocentric down to its innermost core. It differs in this respect from the knowledge of antiquity and the Middle Ages, which was arrived at from the tension existing between man and the physical world (or what is usually inadequately translated as "nature"), between *intellectus* and *esse*. *Physis* and *esse* are the horizon within which the individual can be known, the unseen light by which the existent lights itself and becomes illuminated for the spirit. They are obviously not the nature but the presence of God in the world. As it says in the Psalms, "In thy light (which is not thee, but thy shining for us) we see the light." Being—as the pure mediation between God and the existing things—is the place where the unknown of the divine ground becomes so illuminated for man that "his invisible nature is seen" (Rom 1:20); of course (insofar as it is seen) as something visible (*phaneron*: 1:19), not as in itself but as "understood in the things of creation". This mystery of a God who reveals himself in the world and yet remains unseen, toward whom everything points without his actually appearing, is the basis of the old philosophy. It would be a mistake to suppose that this represented a primitive, half-animistic "divinization of nature", from which biblical and modern technical anthropocentricity has freed us. For it is not primarily a question of nature as the quintessence of the world, but of being, out of which living things are brought forth (*phyo*, *physis*). It is a question of a divine source offering itself to created beings and uncontrollable by man for precisely this reason. It is a mystery reflected in the form of the spirit, but not one that the spirit can claim as its own form. It is rather the mystery of a God transcending the world and yet immanent in the world, a mystery that one may begin to define by the term *analogia entis*, as long as one is clear about what one means by it.

The modern system, which insists on man's ability to control his destiny by means of his intellect, has no place for philosophical mysteries. *Divide et impera* is its slogan, even if the mystery of reality *does* fall uneasily into two halves—with, on the one hand, "What can be known about God" (*gnoston tou theou*: Rom 1:19) and what man can therefore understand and make his own, and, on the other, "what remains unknown" (*aorata*: Rom 1:20) and therefore does not concern man because he has no feeling for it. Hence the movement of modern thought is twofold: first, to bring God closer to man by reducing the difference between them, so that man may appear to assimilate what belongs solely to God; and second, to place

God at such a distance from man that the unknowable part of him is no longer man's concern. This method may be carried out under the names of both Christianity and atheism. By bringing God closer, man sees the importance of the Incarnation; and by removing him to a distance, man treats him with awe and reverence, which will not allow him to be confused with the idols of reason. That is the Christian method. The method of atheism is to bring God so close to man that they become one and the same person, and at the same time to remove God to such a distance that he simply disappears into thin air.

The otherness of God seems to be a new discovery for the present-day Christian. But he has a short memory, for the notion of a God quite different from ourselves was made current by Karl Barth as early as the 1920s. And he was simply renewing the thousand-year-old Christian tradition of apophatic theology, according to which negative statements concerning the possibility of knowing God were considered superior to positive statements (Dionysius the Areopagite and Thomas Aquinas). The apophatic method is not able to establish much similarity between God and his creatures (in the natural and supernatural realms) without discovering the dissimilarity between them to be even greater (Fourth Lateran Council: Denz 432). But the theology of this early period always took into account the mystery of God in its totality, whereas modern theological

thought about the otherness of God defends in the
name of piety (as once Jansenius did) man's right to
experience or think of God as someone very remote.
Why? Three reasons can be given.

1. Because man is determined by his freedom,
which places him, as it does no other creature, vis-à-
vis God. God gives him the freedom to follow his
own devices and to realize to the full his own nature. For this realization he requires an area of freedom in which to move and from which God keeps
himself at a distance. We may say that God lets the
world *be*. This is true in its main sense but not in its
subordinate sense. It is impossible to philosophize by
playing upon words. In addition, it is a very superficial kind of thought that is unable to develop the
basic notion of *analogia entis* to its logical conclusion;
for it is of course also an *analogia libertatis*. The more
completely man participates in God's freedom, the
freer he is, and it is only within the realm of God's
freedom that man can realize his potentiality for
freedom. It becomes clear at the same time that man
cannot stand vis-à-vis God as his "partner", for "he
is the all" (Sir 43:27) and cannot therefore actually
have an opposite number. The old covenant, with
its stressing of man's position as a position in which
he is set over against God, was necessary to counter
the old pantheism, but it is revoked in the christological new covenant (see Gal 3:20ff.). The idea on
which the argument is based is not only anthropo-

centric but anthropomorphic in a somewhat doubtful sense.

2. But the same thinkers can argue their case from a diametrically opposite point of view. God is remote for us because he is not "objective". This is a presupposition of German idealistic philosophy, which claims that there is categorical, objectivizing knowledge (in which categorical form controls matter) and transcendental knowledge, because the spirit becomes indirectly aware of its transcendence over the categorical without this transcendence actually becoming objective. In the final instance the spirit becomes indirectly aware of its own dynamic tendency toward the absolute and of its relation to God, in which God presents himself unobjectively. However important it may be to hold fast to the conception of God as unknowable and unseeable, the objection to this argument is that it ties theology to a one-sided philosophy. Transcendental philosophy exhausts the notion of objectivity in order to develop a philosophy of the intellectual control of the universe and therefore no longer has this notion at its disposal for exploring man's relation to God. In doing so it completely fails to take into account the equally important truth about God that, although "he is the All", he is nevertheless not the world, and consequently, between the two, there exists the primal phenomenon of a relationship in which they are set over against each other. This is analogous to the relationship existing

between the I and the Thou, and also to the divine mystery of the relationship existing among the three Persons, which is the ultimate root of all other objectivity.

3. However, the decisive argument for the distancing of God is not transcendental philosophy but rather its practical effects in a "hominized world". The man who considers and treats the world—animal, vegetable, mineral, sidereal—as simply a quarry for the building of his own house will hardly be likely to see it as a reflection, however pale, of God's image. He has become *homo faber* once again, and the Greek and medieval ages of contemplation (an activity that yields no material profit) lie far behind him. Paul, who was able to perceive clearly God's "eternal power and deity . . . since the creation of the world . . . in the things that have been made", is our witness of this lost world. We ourselves are no longer capable of such witness. We have neither the talent nor the time. We are obliged to make a virtue of necessity and to convert the inability of modern man "to seek God and see if he cannot find him or feel his presence, who is never far from any of us" (Acts 17:27) into a nervous awe of a remote, undiscoverable God whose presence we can never hope to feel. We could, of course, envy the ancients their peculiar gifts and insights, but it is easier to consider their awareness of God's presence as something belonging to a "mythological view of the

world" that we can demythologize to our own advantage. It is, after all, a sign of virtuousness not to want to have too easy a time of it. And because modern man obviously does not have too easy a time of it, the Christian joins modern man and becomes, along with him, one seeking God rather than appear to be one who, naïvely and incredibly, has found God already.

But there is another side to this argument. God revealed himself to mankind in Jesus Christ. Christ brought God close to us—and not only that, for, in doing so, he revealed to us who man in truth really is. He rescued man from his alienation from God and thereby from man himself. It is therefore up to man to make his very own what God gave of himself to the world in the person of Jesus Christ, and to the very last degree, because this is what has become formative of man. Christ intercedes in the affairs of man to bring man to himself, and the greatness of the eighteenth-century Age of Enlightenment, whose tradition was continued by the German Idealists, lies in the fact that it was able to make full use of Christology in the interests of anthropology. Kant very seriously applied himself to doing just that in his "religion within the limits of human reason", and Fichte followed him along the same path with equal seriousness. In the history of mankind, Christ represents the breakthrough from a state of alienation from God (sin) to that of perfect freedom, accomplished in progressive stages throughout history. Quite rightly, therefore, says Fichte, historical time is reckoned by man as coming before or after the appearance of Christ.

It will be necessary to discuss in more detail the "anthropologizing" of Christology, because it deserves special attention as the *pièce de résistance* of the whole process. It provides the bridge between the most authentic Christian thought of the New Testament and atheism, which passes over the bridge without being aware of it, having a share in the central truth of Christianity. It is here that the vital, moving contact point has long existed between the so-called Christian orthodoxy and all the liberal playforms of Christianity. This becomes for us one reason for observing the matter carefully.

First of all, however, it is necessary to ask another question closely allied to the problem of "the halving of the mystery". "In the beginning God created heaven and earth." What is the "heaven" mentioned in this very first passage of the Scriptures? It occurs again and again and with increasing emphasis from the beginning to the end of the Bible. God descends from heaven, looks down on mankind from heaven and vanishes up to heaven with his prophets. Jesus prays to his "Father in heaven" that his will may be done "on earth, as it is in heaven". He ascends into heaven and sends his Spirit down from heaven. According to Peter and Paul our home is in heaven, and it is from heaven that, at the very end, the bride of the Lamb, "the holy city of Jerusalem", "our free mother above", will descend to earth (see Gal 4:24). What kind of a reality is this? At first it appears to be a cosmological reality, for the "firmament" that divides the waters into those above and below it and in which God later places the great lights is called "heaven" by God (Gen 1:8). But it is simply a metaphorical starting point, the significance of which decreases as God's heaven becomes more thickly "populated". This heaven is not God himself, for God created it. But neither does it belong to the developing world of the material cosmos. It is rather the realm or "world" of God, which exists in tension with the realm or world of man. "The heavens are the Lord's heavens, but the earth he has given to the sons of men" (Ps 115:16). It is between these two "realms" or "worlds" that the whole action that the Scriptures describe as revelation takes place, and not between a God without a realm or world of his own and a world of which man is the sole center. The anthropocentric world exists in a state of lively exchange with the theocentric world, and the area of tension between them is the place where the Incarnation, the history of the Church (with the interaction between the earthly and the heavenly Church) and the history of the world (whose true dimensions the prophet of the Apocalypse describes) are all enacted. On the one hand, a final prospect opens up "'a new heaven and a new earth"; but on the other, God's "descent from heaven" of the heavenly Church and so the fulfillment of the prayer "on earth as it is in heaven" becomes the unity of the two that is ultimate fulfillment.

What is modern man to do with such basic and uncompromising assertions as these? The most we could expect of him is to accept the possibility of a spiritual dimension of the material cosmos, which the idea of the Resurrection of Christ and the promised awakening of the dead on the day of judgment seem to demand—in fact, a world ripening under the sun of divine grace toward an ultimate kind of transcendental existence. Yet this does not seem to satisfy all the promises made in the Scriptures. For from the beginning of revelation there exists an increasing openness of heaven over the earth, which is independent of the earth, an abiding accompaniment of earthly events by heaven; and, conversely, earth has increasing access to heaven. There is not a single, lonely God in one Person engaged in a dialogue with mankind, but rather a whole "world of God" engaged in an exchange with the "world of man". All the cosmological undertones that we find in the concretizing imagery of the Psalms have disappeared by the time Christ and his apostles begin to speak. What these have to say is theologically contained within itself.

For the Scriptures, heaven is the realm of mediation between the God "who dwells in unapproachable light, whom no man has ever seen or can see" (1 Tim 6:16) and the world of man. In heaven God's face shall be seen (Rev 22:4), he shall be seen as he is (1 Jn 3:2) and we shall understand fully, even as we have been fully understood (1 Cor 13:12). The promise is of a great world full of love and joy: "You have come . . . to the city of the living God, the heavenly Jerusalem, and to innumerable angels in festal gathering, and to the assembly of the first-born who are enrolled in heaven . . . and to the spirits of just men made perfect, and to Jesus, the mediator of a new covenant" (Heb 12:22–24). To halve the mystery is simply to destroy the unity and integrity of this reality or even reject it altogether, and this is perhaps the greatest impoverishment that present-day theology, without fully realizing it, has suffered in its search for contact with modern man. In the Scriptures the experience of God and Christ is undergone within sight of the openness of heaven, of what Ignatius Loyola calls the *curia coelestis*, the court of heaven—in an openness to the whole world of love, which has nothing in common with the impoverished idea of a conscience hidden from all eyes except God's. The state of man as a state open and exposed to the influence of heaven is seen by Paul as a reason for confidently trusting that he himself will one day be numbered among those who are fully "enlightened".

2. *Postponing the Decision*

In the program of "demythologizing" theology and
holy Scripture, of which we have just had an example but which we naturally cannot develop here in all
its ramifications, we observe first that it cannot de-
limit itself. For the concept "myth" as applied to the
Bible can have no clear determination. The reason
for this is that it is based on a double criterion,
which, considering the nature of the document with
which it is dealing, cannot be reduced to a single
unifying criterion. For the term "mythical" is used to
describe not only what is considered as belonging to
an antiquated view of the world, but also what modern man cannot reconcile with his own scientific
view of the world and what seems alien to him. In
the first case, therefore, its use is dictated by a historical and scientific approach to the Scriptures, and in
the second by an existential approach. These are by
no means one and the same thing.

With regard to the first case, we would have to
prove that those things that are considered as belonging to an antiquated view of the world were in fact
things that had exercised a determining influence on
the actual theology contained in the Scriptures. Furthermore, one would have to prove that these things
in the Scriptures that appear to offer certain analogies
with neighboring mythical cultures do not possess
their own special significance in the realm of biblical

revelation. But this cannot be proved. For instance, it cannot be proved that the assertions based on a Ptolemaic view of the world suffer any harm in being replaced by the Copernican view. It is possible to consider the matter questionable whether the disciples who were with the Lord at his Ascension interpreted his disappearance cosmologically. (Heaven is "above", so the resurrected Lord journeyed "upwards".) Or did they rather interpret with a naïve naturalness that contemporary man may still have when he interprets the cosmos—and quite rightly so—as it perceptibly appears to him. Our heads, together with light and space, belong to what is above; our feet, together with what is dark and stifling, belong to what is below. Or would it have been just the same *for us today*, if Christ had chosen to sink into the earth, in order to show men with normal sense perceptions that he was returning to God the Father?

Why should we pretend to be more stupid than we are and give so much thought to such trifling matters, as if the change in man's view of the world since the time of Christ had suddenly brought a good half of biblical revelation toppling down? But then it may be asked: What about the biblical analogies with neighboring mythical cultures? The answer is that there is evidence enough in the Old Testament that its writers were clearly aware of these analogies as false ones and were fighting against them when they forbade all mythical image-making of Yahweh from the time of Moses right down to the prophets. But it may still be asked: What about the use of certain mythical ideas and word-imagery deriving from Ugarit? The answer is that they probably meant about as much to the prophets and the Psalm writers as the world "Luna" meant to Goethe when he used it to address a poem to the moon. Again, it may be asked: What about the winged creatures in Ezekiel's vision, which he must have seen on the temple walls and gates of Babylon? This "must" is pure assumption, and the whole question is therefore of no consequence whatever, unless we think the assumption is sufficient to call into question the validity of the prophet's vision by applying the methods of depth-psychology. Last of all, it may be asked: What about the virgin birth? After all, there are so many myths in which gods make mortal maidens pregnant! The counter-question to this is: Are we dealing with an event in the Egyptian or Hellenistic world, and not in the strict world of Judaism? Are we supposed to imagine ourselves back in an age when it was thought that the ancient Greek mysteries provided the model for the beliefs of the early Church—an age that is well and truly past? Are Catholic theologians becoming so blind that they can no longer see that the conception of Mary as a virgin mother is built into the very fabric of Christian dogma? Or are we to begin trying to distinguish between "theological" and "historical" truth in a religion that is concerned precisely with incarnation and therefore with the historical truth of its central content of belief?

If one proceeds systematically with this line of inquiry, one soon finds oneself in the area of argument influenced by the second criterion—namely, that the Scriptures contain views no longer compatible with the modern view of the world. At the point of transition from the first criterion to the second, the argument is likely to arise that in earlier times man was for the most part unaware of the scientific basis underlying the chain of causes and effects in the material world, and consequently peopled his cosmos with all sorts of spirits, powers, angels and demons who were ready at all times to produce good or evil effects in the world as the mood took them. Most prayers were therefore addressed to them. Belief in these spirits made miracles seem more likely—hence the readiness to believe that anything unusual that happened was a miracle, and hence also the readiness to ascribe miracles to a particular person whose imposing and highly individual mode of behavior had already made a great impression. Let us note carefully, however, that the stories told about Jesus contain no fanciful miracles (unlike the ones that abound in the Apocrypha). On the contrary, they are all flesh-and-blood examples of fundamental truths about God and his actions. The examples of Christ driving unclean spirits out of the sick—which take place in Mark immediately after the announcement of the coming of the Kingdom of God and the first sermon preached in Capernaum "with authority"— are flesh-and-blood examples, charged with meaning, of the clash between the realms of the Holy Spirit (Mk 1:12) and the unclean spirit (Mk 1:23) in the material world. It is the evangelic principle in action and has nothing to do with myth. Moreover, prayers are never offered to spirits in the Bible, only to God.

But there seems to be no turning back once we are launched on this course. One thing gives rise to another, and each becomes progressively more serious. At what point do these disturbing thoughts arise in the minds of Christians and theologians? And to what lengths are they prepared to go in their concern for religious welfare or the honesty that scholarship demands?

Let us anticipate a considerable part of their argument and admit that the old view of the world was restricted not only in its concept of space but also of time, if we compare it with our own, which gives man alone a prehistory of half a million years. The idea that Christ would return to the earth in a matter of years was something that seemed to fit perfectly well into the time scale of the ancient world, especially if one takes into account the apocalyptic mood of the time. But this element of expectation seems also to be something that is branded very deeply into the whole ethos of early Christianity. Is this not an obvious case of the need to "demythologize" in a very drastic manner? The answer is that if we were to try to arrive at a concept of Christ's authentic teachings and actions by extracting them from certain formulations of the evangelists (who undoubtedly hoped for Christ's return to the earth in a matter of years)—such as "no one knows the moment, not even the Son"—the only result would be to discover that a Christian was all the more strongly bound in obedience to await God's time, and that this was to be interpreted neither literally as a timelessness stretching into infinity, nor narrowly, as an eschatological moment.[1] This would in no way affect our conception of the future of the world; nor would it invalidate the idea that Christ and his Church are wanderers and strangers on the earth; even less would it disguise the fact that the course of world history was a progression toward the sovereign and ultimate figure of Christ, who, as the highest idea of God the world possesses, can only be approached but never overtaken by the evolution of any human and worldly power. Since he already represents that which is greater than anything else we can conceive (*id quo maius cogitari nequit*), he is the judge of all history, who both judges and redeems us as he restores us to ourselves. He is the idea toward which we know we can endlessly strive.

But it may be asked whether the biblical view of

[1] See my essay "Glaube und Naerwartung" in *Zuerst Gottes Reich* (1966).

the world—particularly that of the New Testament, which is static on the one hand and dualistic on the other in its concept of heaven and earth, and which has been influenced partly by Platonic and Gnostic thought and partly by the apocalyptic mood of late Judaism—is at all reconcilable with our present dynamic and evolutive view of the world. In early times man yearned to be transposed into another realm of reality without being able to reach it solely by his own efforts—hence all his prayers and possibly even his sense of sin ("our hearts are unquiet"). Today man works toward his future with the knowledge of all the great developments of nature behind him, and he feels justified in controlling his own development and striving for personal fulfillment under the strict law of communal effort and activity, which is seen as a reward rather than a "punishment" and is assumed to do more honor to the Creator than any amount of vain and idle prayer. This argument leads by a natural process to the final question: Is not the idea of a redeemer who descends from the brightness of heaven to the darkness of earth, leaves behind him a little light and then returns once again to his own sphere, a well-known and often recurring expression of a pattern of thought that is determined by the old dualistic view of the world? And is not the description of Jesus as the "Son of God" and finally as "God" himself not simply the application of this way of thinking to a certain historical person with special gifts of discernment? Does not the simple combination of Christ's doctrine of love for God and one's neighbor with his frightful crucifixion itself suggest to man the idea that his suffering and death were undertaken out of love for the redemption of the whole of mankind? And since we have now gone so far, are not the beginnings of the doctrine of the Trinity suggested with almost inevitable logic by the idea that the Son of earth is God who prays to his Father in heaven and proves his identity with him, and that both are of one spirit?

Are we supposed to refute all this, or will the kindly-disposed reader be satisfied with the assurance that it can be done (if indeed it can)? For we are not at all concerned here with the question of apologetics, but rather with describing the most well-traveled roads. We are also concerned with showing that if one intends to be intellectually honest, it is extremely difficult not to be caught and held up somewhere along this thorny hedge of doubts and misgivings. For when we *are* caught and held up, the reasons for our pursuing this particularly difficult path become clear: *we want to shelve or postpone the decision of faith*, at least until scientific and scholarly exegesis has produced some sufficiently clear results. Perhaps one could find a kind of interim solution by saying that all those biblical statements that demand a commitment of our faith contain a truth that is proportionate to both their actual contents and the antiquated mode in which they are expressed, and that in order to recover our belief we need a complete transposition of the contents into a modern (demythologized) mode of expression. Perhaps it is necessary to conceive everything in "analogous" terms.[2]

This would mean that the action of God or the divine Word, which expressed itself long ago as a blood sacrifice offered for all mankind on the Cross, would have to be made clear to us today in some analogous way that spoke to us more directly. Consequently the equivalent of the *Ernstfall* would be—on an analogy with the way the mythologically thinking Christian was moved by the crucified Christ—that I, to the extent that this image brings it home to me, would be just as deeply moved by the action of the Word of God (promising salvation to me).

Exactly what I would be prepared to die for under these circumstances is not very clear. And it would in any case be very difficult to explain to an enemy who was determined to put me up against a wall and shoot me. It would also be very difficult for a missionary to explain his message to African children. He would probably have to abandon the analogy he may have adopted and resort once more to the unambiguity of the old myth, for which one can also die unambiguously. The trouble is that if the content of our belief becomes analogous, the actions that arise from this

[2] See G. Hasenhüttl, "Was will Bultmann mit seinem Entmythologisierungsprogramm?" *Concilium* 2, no. 4 (1966) 257.

belief are also bound to be analogous, and no one who adopted a belief based on the transposed terms just described could possibly claim to possess an unambiguous faith in Christ as it has been understood by the Church for nearly two thousand years.

Even here the *Ernstfall* is the best criterion, because it forces us to face the Christian truth that our readiness to die for Christ is the only adequate response we can make to his willing sacrifice of himself out of love for us. If we doubt his action, then our response naturally becomes doubtful. Nevertheless, this is our criterion insofar as we show by the dedication of our whole lives to Christ that we have understood Christian truth as the highest possible revelation of eternal love, and all the results obtained by a process of demythologization fall to a considerable and clearly definable extent decisively, visibly and measurably short of the divine magnificence of this love.

What I set out in detail in the first volume of my book *Herrlichkeit* need not be repeated here. Suffice it to say that we suffer from a kind of spiritual color-blindness if we are unable to perceive and appreciate the uniqueness and indestructibility of the revelation presented to us in the Old and New Testaments and prefer instead to search myopically for microscopic details because we have lost the "sensorium" for the quality and the relationship of the total form. It was also portrayed in *Herrlichkeit* how the vision of the glory of God in its revelation is the only way to

avoid having to suspend the assent of faith while serious research is carried out on the Bible. For there is
no doubt that we have to be thankful for biblical research, which has enriched our understanding of revelation and given it a three-dimensional quality. But
in order to be aware of this quality and to be able to
convey this awareness to others, the biblical scholar
needs to be constantly sensitive to the uniqueness of
what he is studying if he is not to fall prey to the
dangers of the demythologizing method. If the
founder of this fundamentally Protestant method un-
dertook his work in order to penetrate to the time-
less core of revelation by stripping it of all the
ephemeral and confusing layers of skin that had
grown over it during the centuries, one ought to
give Goethe's words—"nature has neither core nor
skin"—their due and apply them on a higher level.
The love of Christ is not only the inner core, and the
blood of Christ is not only the outer skin; faith is
founded on the unity of the two. And for this reason
it is not possible to shelve or postpone the decision to
an assent of faith.

3. *The Identification*

I don't know, says the modern Christian, whether I
should get involved with this whole business of the
Ernstfall. For one thing, the Chinese won't be com-

ing for a bit, and then Christianity is a religion of life,
not of death. It's what I really do in everyday life that
counts, not what I imagine I might do when death
comes. Isn't the old saying true: If the small decisions
are taken correctly, the big ones take care of themselves? If I try to live as honestly and decently as I
can, the right attitude will come when I'm dying. If
the catchword of the Reformation was "faith" (and
we know what that led to: Christians made martyrs
of one another for a hundred years), "the love of
one's neighbor" could be the truly effective key moral of today.[3] If this were true, then the whole problem of the *Ernstfall* would be completely different.
The decision for me would not be a decision to be
taken before the Cross of Christ, where a "naked
faith", a *sola fides*, is asked of me. It would be where
it is for every man: in the relationships with his
neighbor, between the alternatives of egoism and
love.

Karl Rahner frees us from a nightmare with his
theory of the anonymous Christian who is dispensed,
at any rate, from the criterion of martyrdom and nevertheless thereby has a full claim to the name of
Christian if he, consciously or unconsciously, gives
God the honor.[4] For "whenever man performs a
positive moral action, fully involving his own power
of free self-determination, the latter is then a positive

[3] K. Rahner, *Schriften zur Theologie*, 6:297.
[4] Ibid., 6:550.

supernatural saving action, in the actual order of salvation, if its *a posteriori* object and the motive, expressly given *a posteriori*, do not obviously come from
the positive revelation of the word, but are, in this
sense 'natural'." Whenever, then, "there is an absolute moral commitment of a positive kind in the
world, given the present order of salvation, there is a
saving event . . . an act of *caritas* is performed." [5]

Of course, this does not free the anonymous
Christian from the duty of trying to discover in
history that "decisive existential of human life:
Christ", [6] which he already has within himself, unconsciously, transcendentally, in an unobjective way,
thus passing into a "higher phase of development of
this Christianity." [7]

But this is then only "the objective and conceptual
statement of what this man has already performed in
the depths of his mental being". [8] It is simply "asked
of him, first, because of the incarnational and social
structure of grace and of Christianity and, secondly,
because to understand it more clearly and purely
reflectively would offer the greater chance of salvation for the individual man." [9] But however desirable, it does not seem indispensable.

[5] Ibid., 6:285–86; 5:221.

[6] "God and the grace of Christ are in everything as the secret essence
of all changeable reality": Rahner, *Schriften*, 4:153.

[7] Ibid., 5:155.   [8] Ibid.

[9] Ibid., 5:156.

This can be proved theologically by highlighting the "radical identity" [10] of the love of God and one's neighbor precisely as the central message of Christ. According to him, the commandments are alike (Mark 12:31 and parallels); they are together the epitome of the Old Testament, and, in the judgment, the "love of one's neighbor will be the only criterion for admittance to the Kingdom of God" (Mt 25:34ff.). Paul emphasizes these statements several times, and, according to John, we are loved by God (Jn 14:21) and Christ, *so that* we can love one another (Jn 13:34), which love is the *new* commandment of Christ (Jn 13:34), that for him is specific (Jn 15:12) and is what is asked of us (Jn 15:17). And so for John the consequence that God, who is love (1 Jn 4:16), *has* loved us, *is not that we love him back* [11] but that we should love *one another* (1 Jn 4:7, 11). For we do not see God; he cannot be truly reached in mystic, Gnostic inwardness in the way that he can be truly reached by love (1 Jn 4:12), and that is why the "God in us" in brotherly love is the God *whom alone we can love* (1 Jn 4:12),[12] so much so that it really is true, and the argument that is absolutely conclusive for John is that "he who does not love his brother whom he has seen, cannot love God whom he has not seen" (1 Jn 4:20).[13]

---

[10] Ibid., 6:282.

[11] My italics.

[12] My italics.

[13] Rahner, *Schriften*, 6:280–81.

By assuming the existence of a supernatural order of grace for all men, as we have said, it follows that all genuine brotherly love is formally and qualitatively the love of God. Even more: because God appears only non-objectively,[14] transcendentally, as a "border experience" in the decisive dependence on other human beings, "categorically explicit brotherly love is the primary act of the love of God",[15] so that, correspondingly, "the thematically religious act as such is secondary in relation to this", although because of its object it has a higher dignity.[16]

This argument is pursued only with the help of the two elements of "moral order" and "supernatural elevation", without any express mention of Christology. At the end it is "pointed out that also the christological . . . side of this situation had to be explicitly considered", but this situation in salvation history obtained for the whole period before the appearance of Jesus, and it is only "radicalized" and "brought to its culmination".[17] This remark makes clear the place of Christ in the comprehensive world plan. If matter and its evolution, stage by stage, exist for the sake of man, in whom creation becomes aware of itself and transcends itself in the direction of God, then, factually, the limitless openness to God, which is the human spirit, exists in order to allow God his ultimate

---

[14] "Not as an object": ibid., 6:293. "God's non-objectivity": ibid., 4:59.
[15] Ibid., 6:295.
[16] Ibid., 6:294.   [17] Ibid., 6:296.

self-expression and self-giving in what is other than himself.[18] The Incarnation of the Logos in *one* human being is an "inner essential element in the engracing of the whole world with God",[19] since this divinization of the world "cannot be at all conceived without this hypostatic union". [20] Christ is "the first step and the lasting beginning and the absolute guarantee that this last self-transcendence, beyond which it is impossible to go, is successful." [21] He is unique; he is also what is to become reality for all mankind. It can be proved (of course only in theological thinking after Christ) that he is the necessary *sine qua non* of the divinization of the world and the "making worldly" of God.[22] He is "the unique *supreme* case of the essential performance of human reality, which consists in the fact that man exists to the extent that he gives himself away".[23] Christ is, by his nature, truly a mediator, more means than an end, a being who makes being possible, a guiding light for all who in the future, in living their own lives, also live according to the final purpose of being: "A person who completely accepts his humanity . . . has accepted the Son of Man, because in him God has accepted man",[24] every man. Because "Christ already stood

[18] Ibid., 5:205.

[19] Ibid., 5:209.   [20] Ibid., 5:208.   [21] Ibid., 5:186–87.   [22] Ibid.

[23] Ibid., 4:142. In vol 3, p. 183, there was mention of the "incommensurable culmination, which is, however, the unique culmination of a creator–creature relationship."

[24] Ibid., 4:154.

within the whole of history as its prospective entele-chy",[25] "Christology is the beginning and end of anthropology"[26] and "all theology is therefore, to all eternity, anthropology".[27]

This is precisely the evolutionistic Christology that Soloviev, basing his thinking on Schelling and Hegel and also on Darwin, presented in the last century as the most modern Christology. For him "the personal embodiment of the Logos in an individual human being is only the last link in a long chain of other physical and historical embodiments; this appearance of God in a physical man is only a more perfect and complete theophany in a succession of imperfect pre-paratory theophanies."[28] Christ is not "something foreign to the general law", but the law of evolution that has come to itself. As Rahner puts it: "If God wants to be non-God, man is born, that and nothing else."[29] "Ultimately human nature is explained in terms of the self-giving self-expression of the Logos itself."[30] But this determines in advance the place of

[25] Ibid., 1:188.

[26] Ibid., 1:205. Cf. 1:184: "Christology as a self-transcending anthro-pology and the latter as a deficient christology".

[27] Ibid., 4:150.

[28] Soloviev, *Lectures on God in Man*, vol. 3, p. 207 (selected works in the German translation by Harry Koehler). Among the twelve types of theology I have treated in *Herrlichkeit*—vol. 2 (1962)—I have dealt with this type, which is so popular today, in tenth place. All the main points made by Teilhard are to be found already in Soloviev.

[29] Rahner, *Schriften*, 4:150.

[30] Ibid., 4:121.

the Cross in this system, of the whole of soteriology. It appears markedly Scotistic: the Incarnation of God as a world goal, even without the fall, certainly not the Incarnation as a function of salvation.[31] Hence, "the mysteries of soteriology can undoubtedly be reduced to the mystery of the Incarnation." [32] This happens in the following way: "Because the world . . . becomes the history of God himself, sin, if and for as long as it is in the world, is enfolded from the beginning by the will to forgive, and the offer of divine self-communication is necessary . . . an offer of forgiveness and the overcoming of guilt. . . . This possibility of forgiveness does not exist by reason of the nature of man, of 'Adam' as such, but through that power of the self-communication of God, which, on the one hand, is behind the evolution of the whole history of the cosmos, but, on the other, is historically tangible as itself and, finding its own goal, is manifest in the existence and life of Christ. *And this is the meaning of the statement that we are redeemed by Christ from our sins.* This is clear from the fact that God's decision in favor of Christ and his saving work supports this saving work and is not supported by it, *that it is not actually the deed of Christ that moves the will of God to forgive, but the deed takes place because of the will.*" [33] It is strange that Rahner, who otherwise

[31] Ibid., 4:160, 170; 5:213.
[32] Ibid., 4:89.
[33] Ibid., 5:215, my italics.

pleads so energetically against Augustine for an economic doctrine of the Trinity, here, when it comes
to the point, speaks only of "God", as if the divine
saving will were not at work here on the Cross between the "allowing" Father and the Son abandoned
by the Father in the form of the Holy Spirit that
unites them both in separating them, so that it becomes a completely obsolete exercise to distinguish
between a "saving will of God toward Christ" and
the "deed of Christ that moves the will of God".
Nor is it relevant, when Rahner is speaking of the
Cross, to engage in a constant polemic against a
legalistic doctrine of satisfaction[34] (thus failing to
understand the ultimate purposes of Anselm), for it is
a question of the interpretation of the statement in
the New Testament that Christ bore our sins on the
Cross. What does it mean? An answer is rightly demanded,[35] but little more is offered as a solution than
the suggestion that we should not take as much notice of the "bitter sufferings" as of the death, which
means with Christ the final acceptance by God.[36]
This is undoubtedly true, but it does not show why
this death in abandonment by God (which only the
eternal Son of God can know in its full depths) had
to follow as the sum of the "bitter suffering". There
is lacking here a theology of the Cross that Rahner

[34] Ibid., 1:213–16; 4:160, 164f.
[35] Ibid., 1:213.
[36] Ibid., 4:165–66.

has not yet given us. It is true, of course, that the emphasis on the doctrine of an anonymous Christianity[37] (with the evolutionary background we have outlined above), so urgently required in the present situation, involves a proportionate devaluation of the theology of the Cross and, correspondingly, of the theology of Christian living in terms of the *Ernstfall*. For, according to what we have said, man does not owe his redemption actually to Christ, but to the eternal saving will of God, which is made manifest to him in the life of Christ. There is no need, then, for the *Ernstfall*, and there is no more talk of it.

This was not always Rahner's emphasis. Once he was a great exponent of the *Ecclesia ex latere Christi* and thus of devotion to the Sacred Heart. This was the real center for him. "This original source of love is the heart of the Lord",[38] and it is "the anxious, exhausted, dead heart". And here was the "essential nature of time" and of the "mission".[39] It was also said that this devotion was an inner balancing out of Ignatian spirituality, which, being based on indifference, risks inducing "an almost overdeveloped sense of the relativity of everything that is not God himself". "Ignatius is the man of transcendental spirituality and not so much of categorical spirituality." [40]

[37] Ibid., 5:522.
[38] *Sendung und Gnade* (1959), p. 533.
[39] Ibid., p. 546.
[40] Ibid., pp. 520, 522.

But now we must really stop for a moment and ask a question. Is, then, devotion to the Sacred Heart a "categorical" supplement to a transcendental spirituality? Or does perhaps this "original source of love" mean also the end of this whole Kantian philosophy? Do I see in the broken heart of the crucified Christ the love of the triune God—or don't I? John says that I see it, although no one has ever seen God. I see it, but not in the way that one can make a categorical synthesis of S and O. Should we not rather reconsider everything that has been said about the "non-objectivity of God" (who alone in our fellowman becomes an object of primary human response), as well as the curious scriptural reference presented to us?

Of course Jesus continues the two commandments of the Old Testament and says the second is like the first. And of course he does it because of his own Incarnation, as the parable of the judgment expressly assumes when it states: "As you did it to one of the least of my brethren, you did it to me." Thus it is a statement that is tied to the synthesis that Jesus Christ represents[41] and therefore cannot be arrived at by an abstract combination of "nature" and "supernature"

---

[41] Although the synthesis might have been prepared for in the contemporary rabbinate (Lk 10:27), with the primacy of the commandment to love God, to transfer this primacy to the love of one's neighbor would certainly amount to an abandonment of the whole theological ethic of the Old Testament.

(morality and *caritas*). Moreover, the Old Testament wording of both parts is very conscious and does not simply disappear within the synthesis, so that, in New Testament terms, it could equally well say: "You should love your neighbor with your whole heart, your soul and your whole mind." In the incarnate Christ we see the overflowing of the totality of what we owe God into Christ's neighbor, essentially because he himself is the neighbor or (as in the parable of the Samaritan) has made himself such with his divine love for us, who are lying half-dead by the wayside. True, the Samaritan is not orthodox, let alone a priest or Levite; he is the typical "heretic" (but not a "pagan") who still does the right thing in spite of his misguided beliefs. But he is, above all, the invention of Jesus Christ, an image of himself, who has brought the fulfillment "outside the camp" of orthodoxy (Heb 13:11–13).

To interpret John and leave out Christ is exegetically unacceptable. As we know, John argues in a circle, and one must keep one's eyes all the time on the whole revolving line of this circle. Everywhere the farewell discourses and the first Epistle assume the direct love of the disciples for Jesus, and it is a love that transcends his humanity—namely, the belief that he is the Son of God: "The Father himself loves you, because you have loved me and have believed that I come from the Father" (Jn 16:27). The phrase "abide in me", repeated six times in the image of the vine, obviously calls for the loving dwelling in the origin of Christian love, so that the Christian receives the new commandment from the mutual love between the disciples and the Lord, again expressed—in a circular way: "If a man loves me, he will keep my Word" (Jn 14:23) and "He who has my commandments and keeps them, he it is who loves me" (Jn 14:21). The proof of their love for the Lord is that the disciples let him go to the Father (Jn 14:28). Nor can the christological implication be excluded for a moment from the Epistle, for the model of love is, expressed positively and negatively, always the love of Christ: "In this is love, not that we loved God but that he loved us and sent his Son to be the expiation for our sins" (1 Jn 4:10). "By this we know love, that he laid down his life for us" (1 Jn 3:16). Thus the identity is there, but only christologically, and with the absolute priority of the love of God (a genitive in both a subjective and an objective sense), which then overflows from God and, together with God, to our neighbor.

The Christ who lives in me is so deeply within me (and closer to me than I am to myself) because he died for me, because he took me to himself on the Cross and constantly takes me to him again in the Eucharist. How could my relationship with my neighbor be comparable to that—and therefore require the same answering love from me? The bridge to brotherly love in the sense of Christ is the fact that he has done for everyone what he has done for me.[42]

What is a Carmelite life? An offer of one's whole being to the God of Jesus Christ, so that he can use this being according to his loving pleasure for the work of salvation. By it we recognize the true identity of brotherly love with the love of God, but not in the way that Rahner describes it; the "religious act as such" is primary.

To miss out the Cross and its whole context also diminishes the importance of sin. A life to expiate the guilt of the world appears, as far as the love of one's neighbors goes, hardly "operative". And who can, after all, "wholly accept his humanity" with that much praised "honesty", with "the courage to do one's daily duty", without encountering his own sin in the process? And what does he do then? Does he forget it? Does he pardon himself for it? Or does he let it be covered by God's comprehensive desire for reconciliation? But what if he has the conscience of a Luther?

---

[42] Of course this is not to deny Karl Rahner's legitimate notion that there is a *fides implicita* and a corresponding supernatural love outside the sphere of Christianity (see Lk 21:1–4) and of the Bible (see Mt 15:21–28), as well as with those who are theoretically atheists (Rom 2:14–16).

4. *Futurism*

With the latest theological catchword: "Retreat to
the front ranks", we have reached the farthest point
of advance, where the great dynamic and evolutive
movement toward the future in the modern view of
the world coincides with the scriptural idea of Exo-
dus, which interprets the fact that the Christian, who
is never at home in this world, is not so in a static
way, but rather dynamically in relation to the messianic eschatological future of the world, to the coming of the Kingdom of God. "Flight from the world"
because one's home is elsewhere—it cannot be denied—is a Christian motive, but it must be a "flight
from the world in hope" and together with the
world (of which the Church is, after all, a part)—
"forward", toward the final fulfillment. And this
hope is not a mere waiting, based on the things of
yesterday and the things of today, the incongruence
of which in the world is experienced by Christians as
painful; rather, this hope must be "productive and
have a fighting spirit", and its pains must be the
birth-pangs of the world as it brings forth this final
birth. We cannot have two ultimate goals before us,
a natural one and a supernatural one. The world that
man has to build with his natural powers is also the
Kingdom of God, the coming of which he has to
help bring about by suffering the birth-pangs (Jn
16:21–22; Rom 8:22–23); because this hope is com-

pletely open to the future and does not have any "scientific" images of the future before it, and not even the image of a progress already achieved, and yet works in service of one's neighbor toward the growth of the Kingdom, defiant of death and hoping against all hope, it is a life lived between the Cross and the Resurrection, involved both eschatologically and in the world, both spiritual and political.

These strains are not new in the history of spirituality and theology. Their ultimate source is undoubtedly late Jewish messianism, which is precisely an attempt to deal with the problems of the gulf between the expectation and the helping to bring about the end (cf., for example, Martin Buber's *Gog and Magog*). The tension can still be felt in the early days of Church theology with Irenaeus [43] and then gets covered over with a kind of Platonism. But it emerges again in the brood of the idealists, who are very important for Soloviev's political theology, in another form in the religious socialism of Kutter and Ragaz and in Karl Barth's first commentary on Romans (1919).

It is theology of the Holy Spirit, just as the great passage on the sighing of creation, especially of the children of God for the redemption of the material world, is to be found in the chapter in Romans on the Spirit. "For we do not know how to pray as we

[43] See *Herrlichkeit*, 2:92–93.

ought" (because we have no images of the future), "but the Spirit himself intercedes for us with sighs too deep for words. And he who searches the hearts of men knows what is the mind of the Spirit, because the Spirit intercedes for the saints according to the will of God" (Rom 8:26–27).

At this point, however, the discerning of spirits comes into its own. There is no doubt that the area that Christian thinking has to accord to the Holy Spirit can never be wide enough. The appearance of Jesus Christ as God on earth in the form of a servant was a short, inconspicuous moment in the history of the world. A few words, a few actions, and it was all over: "It is to your advantage that I go away. . . . When the Spirit of truth comes, he will guide you into all the truth" (Jn 16:7, 13). The tiny revelation of words and deeds opens into dimensions that are known to the Spirit of God alone. He is Spirit, no longer word; he is Freedom, tied to no human philology and exegesis. His interpretations are in principle inconclusive, always new, always surprising, and always greater than the theologians thought. This is always more uncomfortable than a cozy Christianity. Someone who is "in the Spirit" is "removed"; he has lost the ground beneath his feet; he could not be "in the Spirit" if he held on to something. The Spirit is also he who bears witness (Rom 8:16; Jn 5:9–10), and the disciples are witnesses with him (Jn 15:26–27). And if with their life they give a testimony of blood, it seems that they do it in the realm of the Spirit who, when they pray (groaning and sighing for the coming Kingdom of God on earth, without yet having any knowledge of it), supports their prayer, full of knowledge, with his witness and his sighs. It is a prophetic witness and martyrdom, no longer bound to that distant historical past of the Cross and the death of Jesus, not bound by one foot to the tether of a historical facticity, but in the free responsible choice to take upon itself the birth-pangs in the world of "the glory that is to be revealed to us" (Rom 8:18). If this kind of man of the Spirit becomes a martyr, then he is a martyr of the coming kingdom, of which he cherishes within himself a great and more open expectation than those who kill him.

But he is not a martyr of Christ. His martyrdom is not a response to the martyrdom of Christ, who died for him. Of the Spirit, which will lead us into all truth, it is written: "He will not speak on his own authority, but whatever he hears he will speak, and he will declare to you the things that are to come. He will glorify me, for he will take what is mine and declare it to you" (Jn 16:13–14). These words are paradoxical, for if the Spirit does not speak on his own authority, but has to listen in order to be able to speak, it seems that, when he hears the things of Christ, he hears them as past things and is not able to declare the things that are to come. But that is precisely what it is said he does do. When the Spirit imparts his knowledge, it is Christ that he glorifies. There is no independent glorification in which the Spirit would reveal his own searches into the depths of the Godhead (1 Cor 2:10), and if he leads the world to a glory that is to come (Rom 8:18) and to the "glorious liberty of the children of God" (Rom 8:21), then that will be again the glorification of Christ. So Christ is the one who is coming, inasmuch as he is the explicated one who has come—*videbunt in quem transfixerunt*. [44]

This is the point at which the decision is made as to whether the "retreat to the front ranks" is ultimately a flight from the Cross or a flight to it, whether these pangs of a world being born in the Holy Spirit are ultimately the explanation of the Cross given by the Spirit—in the sense of completing what is lacking in Christ's sufferings (Col 1:24) and of the birth-pangs until Christ has taken shape in the world (Gal 4:19)—or whether it is a cosmological or pneumatological process, in which the spirit of mankind fights its way out of alienation to its own authenticity. And even if we think of the second as integrated within the first, the criterion of the Christianity of the whole would still be the *Ernstfall*.

[44] It is not without reason that these words are quoted in the Book of Revelation. The one book of the Bible and of the Christian heritage that deals with the future makes the closest connection between the prophecy of the Spirit and martyrdom (e.g., Rev 18:24); martyrdom, however, is always the testimony of a death died for Christ (Rev 6:9; 7:14; 12:17; 18:24; 19:10; 20:4).

But every Christian plan of the future will, and must, be valueless if it does not remain Christian, that is, oriented toward Christ. For Christ is not a "program" that can be surveyed or drawn off and bottled and simply taken with one on a "future operation". Only in the openness of contemplation and listening prayer is there revealed to us ever anew what Christ, in whom we have our origin, means and wants. Every action that is not rooted in contemplation is doomed to sterility from the start.

5. *We Anonymous Atheists and Our Dialogue*

We have now taken up the argument on all the levels mentioned and confronted it with the *Ernstfall*. But there is not always someone to take it up in this way. And principles (especially if they are presented in the form of catchwords), once proclaimed, tend automatically to produce consequences. Anyone who uses catchwords in this way is responsible for their being received in their crude poster-like form, without the learned commentaries he gives on them that are a protection and a qualification. The title is enough for most people; it becomes independent and does not need the subsequent treatise in order to have its effect. One cannot say that one did not mean this to happen. Anyone who uses the phrase "demythologization of the Bible" is understood to mean that the

Bible is mythical. To what extent, as far as the people who hear him are concerned, is a second and far less important question. Anyone who says he is pursuing "theology as anthropology" is saying that every statement made about God in this study is also, in the same way, said of man; but he is silently leaving the presupposition of all theology in the shade: namely, that it is the Logos of a God who speaks to man. Man is listening and is not himself already speaking. The "logy" part of the word, which appears quite unambiguous, in fact obscures. Anyone who speaks of "anonymous Christians" cannot avoid (nor doubtless would he want to) the conclusion that there is ultimately no difference between Christians who are such by name and Christians who are not. Hence—despite all subsequent protests—it cannot matter whether one professes the name or not. And anyone who proclaims the identity of the love of God and one's neighbor and presents the love of one's neighbor as the primary meaning of the love of God must not be surprised (and doubtless is not) if it becomes a matter of indifference whether he professes to believe in God or not. The main thing is that he has love. Admittedly, this is true if he knows what love is. But by what criterion does a man who is essentially a sinner measure love? Surely by what, with some effort, he is still capable of doing. Is this criterion enough and can it (with God's grace) be interpreted as *caritas*? "In this is love, not that we loved God . . ." (1 Jn

4:10). "But God shows his love for us in that while we were yet sinners Christ died for us" (Rom 5:8). This takes the criterion of love from us, so that we give God the honor and are measured according to his measure; this requires of us that we also should give our life for our brothers (1 Jn 3:16). But a person who does this assuredly knows God alone.

A theology that develops from catchword principles is always a theology that levels out, mitigates and cheapens, and finally liquidates and sells out. Whether it wants to or not, it asymptotically approaches atheism. Now this approach was the first possible decision in the alternative we originally proposed. Of course, there are two reasons for this movement. One is weariness with the form of faith hitherto and the need to find at last something simpler, more comprehensible and more suited to the man of today. Let us leave on one side for a moment this motive, which we find everywhere. The second reason is the human and Christian need for dialogue, which, at the highest level, is a dialogue with atheism. If one were to succeed in reducing the whole of Christianity to humanism and at the same time have the comfortable feeling that one had, by compression, accommodated the maximal within the minimal point (namely, the love of God in the love of one's neighbor) so that the dialogue with atheism could take place from the center of Christian truth, then what we could offer in dialogue from our side would be complete. But whereas we, most honestly, are able to address our partners in dialogue as anonymous Christians, if they behave decently and according to their conscience, and God places an extra supernatural value on their virtues and interprets them as faith, hope and love, they will undoubtedly accord us an equal right and greet us as anonymous atheists, since our so-called dogmatic theology is simply an ideological superstructure above a common, or garden, humanism and its anthropology. Are they wrong? It all depends. On what? The *Ernstfall*. But simply to die —however impressive its effect may sometimes be at the time—surely, in human terms, breaks off the dialogue. And yet dialogue is what is asked of us. Thus we must face the question: What form should it take on the Christian side?

In the humanism that Christianity is supposed to be, all that God has given in his revelation of the world would also have to be visible.[45] If we succeeded in making Christian life a function of the revelation to the world, then something of the Word of God to the world could be heard through us. Our starting point would not be human, but divine, inter-subjectivity, into which man is admitted through the opening of the Trinity in the Incarnation. This happens in Jesus Christ, who invites us to call, with him, the trinitarian Father "Abba" by bearing our sins

[45] For the following, see *Glaubhaft ist unsere Liebe* (1963), pp. 75ff.; *Das Ganze im Fragment* (1963).

(which prevent us from saying "Father") and to follow his way of life of complete poverty and complete
obedience in an attitude of, in its highest form, even
physical chastity. For he gives his Father honor by
opening up every area in himself to the richness and
the will of the Father—and this whether he works as
a carpenter for thirty years or preaches for a few
months. The boundless openness to his Father, which
one might call Christ's confessional attitude, makes it
possible for him to bear within him to the Father his
brother, who has cut himself off from him, and to
open him up, as he does so, through suffering, in a
hidden and lonely place of which the sinner knows
nothing and which is not "dialogical". Thus only one
particular level of the relation between Christ and his
neighbor—and that not the most important—will be
devoted to dialogue. The more essential thing takes
place in prayer, the dimensions of which stretch as far
as abandonment on the Cross. From the opened
Trinity, which is made available to us in the opened
broken heart on the Cross, there streams forth the
tremendous mystery of everlasting love, and, over-
whelmed by it, the Christian gives his heart to his
brother—boundlessly, even to the point of dying for
him. At a superficial level he is in dialogue with him,
in a movement of affecting him by his words and being affected by *his*; but at a deeper level he is, in relation to his brother, already at that point where at the
Cross all dialogue between Christ and men is broken

off because Christ now bears all men within him and they kill him. Death is now the action, a death in silence. At a superficial level the Christian can shake the dust from his feet and go on (Mt 10:14), but at a deeper level he is carrying his friend or his opponent within himself in such a way that he could wish himself "accursed and cut off from Christ for the sake of my brethren, my kinsmen by race" (Rom 9:3). This bearing quality in all dialogue is not dialogic, and one's partner does not even need to be told of it. The theoretical quality that distinguishes the humanism of the Christian from every other, in actual fact, enters the sphere of the dialogue only as a borderline phenomenon, a readiness for the *Ernstfall*. And now a strange thing happens: it is precisely the readiness, beyond the dialogue, to go much further with one's brother than one can go even in the dialogue that opens the Christian heart to the best possible and longest dialogue. The Christian lets himself be involved more deeply than anyone else because his partner, perhaps his opponent, is, like himself, someone who is also borne in the crucified Heart. For reasons of prudence he can adjourn a dialogue, but he cannot finally break it off. For in the Cross the dividing wall that separates the speakers at the moment has already been torn down (Eph 2:14)—not by talking, but through the most lonely suffering.

But should not the whole world of the Church be able to be integrated like this? Undoubtedly—and

here we obtain valuable criteria for the true significance and range of Vatican Council II. But these
criteria are again subject to our other criterion,
which can ultimately determine the extent to which
they point to renewal or a leveling out. The Church
must always "be the resplendence of the glory of
Christ for all men" (*Constitution on the Church,* no. 1),
and glory in Scripture is the eternal love that radiates
from the union of the Cross and the Resurrection. In
her sacramental, constitutional and existential community elements, the Church must be the true and
credible presentation to the whole world of the trinitarian christological mystery; everything within her
must be for all men; all her paths should, like those of
the heavenly Jerusalem, be of "transparent gloss" on
which the stream of living water "flows crystal clear"
(Rev 21:21; 22:1–2).This is much more difficult than
the construction of a building that is autistically shut
within itself. The Council has undoubtedly made
Church matters more difficult. Those who seek miti-
gations in everything and express delight at the
"progress" and the growing "maturity" as each barrier falls do not understand what the Fathers were
concerned with. It was to direct into the secular
world through the Church, which is a divine mystery, the mysterious ray of trinitarian and crucified
love, wholly and completely. Let us add that this image of the Church—the mediation of the *whole* love
of God to the *whole* world—is what makes possible

true love of our neighbor. The barrier must fall that Augustine set up through his concept of a double predestination to heaven and hell: that everyone can ultimately hope for himself only. No, on the contrary, I must be able to hope for every brother so much that, in a fictitious *Ernstfall*, if it were a question of whether he or I were to enter into the Kingdom of God, I would—with Paul (Rom 9:3)—let him go. But in order to know what that means, one would have to have uppermost in his mind a theology of Holy Saturday—the descent of Christ into hell—or at least a theology of the dark night of the soul of which John of the Cross gave an experimental description. But who today has time to worry about such things?

This would be the way in which a Christian would have to start a dialogue with the non-Christian if he does not want to show himself wholly unworthy of his name. He does not put the content of his faith in parentheses; he does not water it down to a bland and shallow humanism, but accepts the responsibility for it and represents it with the grace of God in the situation of his mission. He is full of confidence that this is possible: "Do not be anxious how you are to speak or what you are to say . . . for it is not you who speak, but the Spirit of your Father speaking through you" (Mt 10:19–20). But this means, in precise terms: Stop those barren transpositions of the mysteries of God into modern nursery rhymes; the Word of my Father is not suited for a Play Bach. Compose for me no more basic theology for which God no longer provides the yardstick but rather the alleged partner in dialogue, and which really springs only from your anxiety about being on top of the times (and which unveils your role-conscious pride). Believe instead what I promised you: that the Spirit of your Father will be sufficient for you to deal with your "situations".

6. *When the Salt Loses Its Savor*

Like a house that has vanished, so is wisdom to a fool; and the knowledge of the ignorant is unexamined talk.
—Sirach 21:18

The well-disposed commissar: Comrade Christian, can you tell me frankly what you Christians are up to? What are you still doing in our world? What do you see as the justification for your existence? What's your job?

The Christian: First of all, we are men like any other men who are helping to build up the future.

The Commissar: I accept your first statement, and I hope that the second is true.

The Christian: We have recently become "open to the world", and some of us even have become seriously converted to the world.

The commissar: That sounds like crafty priests' talk. It would be even better if, as "men like any other men", you had first become converted to an existence that is worthy of man. But to the point. Why are you still Christians?

The Christian: Today we are Christians come of age. We think and act on our own moral responsibility.

The commissar: I hope so, if you say you are men. But don't you have some special belief?

The Christian: That's not so important. The main thing is the morality appropriate to the age. Today's emphasis is on brotherly love. He who loves his neighbor loves God.

The commissar: If he existed. But since he does not exist, you do not love him.

The Christian: We love him inclusively, unobjectively.

The commissar: Ah, so your belief is without an object. We're making progress. Things are getting clearer.

The Christian: It's not quite so simple as that. We believe in Christ.

The commissar: I've heard of him. But it seems we know little about him historically.

The Christian: Granted. Virtually nothing. That is why we believe less in the historical Jesus than in the Christ of the kerygma.

The commissar: What's that word? Chinese?

The Christian: Greek. It means the proclamation of
the Gospel. We feel that the linguistic event of the
Gospel of faith concerns us.

The commissar: And what does this Gospel state?

The Christian: It depends on the effect it has on you.
It can promise you the forgiveness of sins. This, at
any rate, was the experience of the original Christian community. It must have been led to this
conclusion through the events surrounding the
historical Jesus, of whom we do not actually know
enough to be certain that he . . .

The commissar: And you call this "conversion to the
world"? You Christians are still just as obscurantist
as you always were. And you want to help build
up the world with that kind of wishy-washy talk!

The Christian (playing his last trump): We have Teilhard de Chardin. He has a great influence in Po-
land!

The commissar: We have him ourselves already. We
did not need to get him from you first. But it's a
good thing that you've finally got that far. Just
throw out all that mystical hocus-pocus, which has
nothing to do with science, and then we can start
talking about evolution together. We'll forget
about the other stories. If you yourselves know so
little about them, you are no danger to us. You'll
save us a bullet or two. In Siberia we have some
very useful camps. There you can prove your love
of humanity and work away at evolution. You'll

achieve more than you do here in your university chairs.

The Christian (somewhat disappointed): You're underestimating the eschatological dynamism of Christianity. We are preparing the way for the coming of the Kingdom of God. *We* are the true world revolution. Equality, Liberty, Fraternity: that is our real concern.

The commissar: A pity that others had to fight the battle for you. It's easy to associate yourself with something after the event. Your Christianity is not worth its salt.

The Christian: You are associated with us! I know who you are. You are a decent fellow. You are an anonymous Christian.

The commissar: Don't be stupid, my friend. Now I've understood enough. You've liquidated yourselves and spared us the trouble of persecuting you. Dismissed!

IV

Cordula

When the Huns caught sight of the young girls they fell upon them with savage howls, like wolves among sheep, working havoc among them and destroying them all.

But there was one girl called Cordula, who out of fear hid herself the whole night long in a ship. The following morning, however, she offered herself up to the fury of the Huns, and thus received the crown of martyrdom. Afterward, her feast day was not celebrated because she had not suffered together with the others. A long time afterward, therefore, she appeared in a vision to a woman hermit and asked for her death to be commemorated on the day after the feast of the eleven thousand virgins.

—*The Legend of the Eleven Thousand Virgins*

What then should a Christian be? He should be one who offers up his life in the service of his fellow man because he owes his life to Christ crucified. But what does he possess of such worth that he can give to his fellow men? Certainly not visible things. The gift he has to give—that which was given him by God—is deeply rooted in the unseen and invisible nature of God. "For you have died, and your life is hid with Christ in God" (Col 3:3). If a Christian were to imagine that he could make visible and give to his fellow

men all the qualities he possesses, he would simply become mere surface and would no longer have anything deeper to offer. There are of course things that
it is possible for him to give and make manifest, but
these things are not exactly those which help to give
shape to the visible Church, such as divine service,
Church festivals, the sacraments and the sacral posts of
office. It is rather the seed of the divine life, which,
channeled through these things, germinates and blos-
soms in the individual Christian. These gifts are
difficult to grasp, since they are more like a fragrance
wafted toward us from God than anything tangible.
"For we are the aroma of Christ to God . . ." (1 Cor
2:15). Paul seeks to describe the garden of love, which
here bursts forth into new life, with many different
names: "Compassion, kindness, lowliness, meekness,
patience, forbearing one another . . . the peace of
Christ . . . and above all these put on love" (Col 3:12–
15). And again: "Love, joy, peace, patience, kindness,
goodness, faithfulness, gentleness, self-control" (Gal
5:22), in connection with which it is important to observe that joy is mentioned immediately after love,
and that from this joy should emanate, like the fragrance from flowers, all the various kinds of love and
forgiveness that are a reflection of that love vouchsafed to Christians (Col 3:13) by Christ himself and
therefore by God (Eph 4:32)—"a fragrant offering and
sacrifice to God" (Eph 5:2). "Rejoice! let all men
know your forbearance. . . . Have no anxiety about

anything" (Phil 4:4–6). Joy in defenselessness, defenselessness without anxiety: in these words a mysterious superiority makes itself felt. Behind the beatitudes of the Sermon on the Mount, with its glorification of the meek, the gentle, the merciful, the peaceful and the lowly—behind the command not to resist or retaliate in the face of persecution lies the idea of joy as the fountain that nourishes all since the resurrection of the Lord. Stephen dies joyfully, with a vision of heaven opening to receive him. Paul looks forward to death in a state of joyfulness and invites us all to rejoice with him at the prospect (Phil 2:17–18). With the knowledge that heaven is open to receive him and that it is the heart of all things laid open, the Christian is nourished even in his ordinary day-to-day life by a never-failing fountain, which springs from the very depths of God's nature and wells up in his servants into eternal life (Jn 4:14).

In this outpouring of love lies God's unequivocal affirmation of all things, and we Christians must and ought to respond with an equally unequivocal "Amen" (2 Cor 1:18–20). Our affirmation of existence should be absolute, not restricted, and it should be of such a kind that it does not make us feel the need to silence our opponents at all costs, like Nietzsche, nor take refuge in utopian visions of the future, like Bloch, simply because the present is not perfect. There is nothing wholly negative apart from sin, and this is borne in the heart of our Lord. All suffering, even the darkest night of the crucifixion, is encompassed by a joy that may possibly remain unfelt but is affirmed and made known through faith. In the final instance, this joy is what moved Cordula to come out of her hiding place in the belly of the ship. She had to hurry in order to catch up with her friends. For during the course of the night spent lying in the ship she came to understand something— the same thing Jonah came to understand in the belly of the whale: that death is what gives life its form and shape. Before such a moment of understanding, one is never quite sure. We know it, however, and shall know it to the end of the world, by the testimony of the thief on Christ's right hand. Could it be that the Christian has the unprecedented opportunity of giving form and shape to his life through an awareness or foreknowledge of its final shape, so that one could know from the very beginning who he is? Cordula, on the other hand, had to hurry in order not to miss this opportunity. To be commemorated a day later than the others was not so important, but it was important to be included with the others. It was, after all, a matter of a feast day, and feast days are days of rejoicing. Neither the one who celebrates it nor the one whose death it commemorates bears weapons; each is defenseless. And this defenselessness is what really matters.

If one questions the outcome of Vatican Council II (and what that is depends to a large extent on us), the answer should surely be this. We have said already that it should be the Church's defenseless exposure of herself to the world, the dismantling of all bastions and the leveling of all bulwarks to boulevards. And it must take place without any mental reservations or secret hopes of a new triumph, since our discovery that the old kind of triumph is no longer practicable or desirable. We must not imagine that we can make the entry into a heavenly Jerusalem with a waving of palms and seated on the gentle ass of evolution, even though those old war-horses, the Holy Inquisition and the Holy Office, have been abolished. Defenselessness in the face of the world means above all the relinquishing of a security system that man imposes and controls between the realms of the natural and the supernatural by means of a metaphysical panoramic view of the universe stretching from Alpha (or, rather, Atom) to Omega. For it is absolutely certain that in such a system the supernatural will soon be reduced to a function of the natural. Nature is always first in the arena with its laws, structures, and postulates. We are prepared to accept and understand all such things, and as a result we have a kind of inner understanding for matters concerning grace. They become necessary in order to complete or at least rectify the course begun by nature, and they interpose themselves into the process more or less as a means of achieving the goal. (Without the Incarnation, evolution will not arrive at its completion, nor will man be raised to the point of beholding God.) Man frequently doctors up what the Word of God can and must say, thereby erecting bastions that are all the more dangerous for being more subtle.

The Christian must naturally be forever trying to define and determine his position anew in order to pray and act in the right way. He comes by way of God to his fellow Christians, and he looks with his fellow Christians toward God—that is, on the way of Christ to God and not simply on the world's way to God. But the curve or arc that the path of Jesus describes cannot be gauged by us, for the very reason that the experience of the crucifixion, hell and the resurrection lay on the way and separates us from it like an abyss. But neither can the curve of the Christian's path be gauged, and for that reason he can dispense with care and allow God to place him in a defenseless position. It goes without saying, and is deserving of no particular praise, that as a man among other men he should feel himself duty bound to work with them to achieve a common goal, both in the present and in the future. "If anyone will not work, let him not eat" (2 Th 3:10). It is superfluous to consider the Christian "openness to the world" as especially praiseworthy, because Christians are themselves a part of the world and should not act or behave differently from anybody else. They are different only in the sense that they are something else besides this, which cannot be fitted into what is called the "world". For they are there to bear witness to the love of God and, if they have a mind to, let this love shine through them into the world. Their task is to testify (if necessary by the sacrifice of their own lives) that this love is the eternal life that triumphs over death. They do not seek death, although the desire for martyrdom may not be unknown to them. They may be placed somewhere between the first and the second Ignatius—and the second Ignatius adopted this name out of reverence for the first. The first hastened toward his death joyfully, and all that we possess of him lies in the running toward this involuntary and yet cherished death.

What an epitaph! *Aere perennus!* "Let me be given to the wild beasts, for through them I can attain unto God. . . . Rather entice the wild beasts that they may become my sepulcher, and may leave no part of my body behind, so that I may not, when I am fallen asleep, be burdensome to anyone. Then shall I be truly a disciple of Jesus Christ, when the world shall not so much as see my body. . . . Now I am learning in my bonds to put away every desire. . . . It is good for me to die for Jesus Christ rather than to reign over the farthest bounds of the earth. Him I seek who died on our behalf; him I desire who rose again for our sake. The pangs of a new birth are upon me. . . . Suffer me to receive the pure light, when I am come thither; then I shall be a man. Permit me to be an imitator of the Passion of my God. If any man hath him within himself, let him understand what I desire. . . . Rather stand ye on my side—that is, on God's side. Speak not of Jesus Christ and withal desire the world. . . . I write to you in the midst of life, yet lusting after death. My lust hath been crucified. . . . Entreat ye for me, that I may attain [through the Holy Spirit]" (St. Ignatius, *Epistle to the Romans*).

The second Ignatius heard all that and so adopted the name. Over his maxim he writes: "Jesus, my beloved, is crucified." But he was not in any sense "in bonds", and he was aware that he had no right to seek out a death for himself when God required him to live and be active in his cause. The literalness with which the first Ignatius understands and answers the call to death by martyrdom becomes for the second Ignatius a challenge to use every moment of his existence to the full in the service of the Lord. It is not necessarily physical death that matters above all else, but rather that we should sacrifice our lives daily for our Lord and our brethren and, in the process, become so completely submerged in the ordinary and the commonplace that even words begin to sound much too loud. One can stop using them altogether and forget. It is all irrelevant. In his *sume et suscipe* the second Ignatius continually implores the divine fire to seize hold of him, ravish and consume him. "Whatever I am, whatever I possess—freedom, memory, understanding, will, body—it all belongs to thee; it all stems from thee, and to thee I return it; dispose of it as thou wilt, for thine own sake and not for mine. And in its stead let thy love and grace live in me, so am I satisfied." Martyrdom means bearing witness. It is not so very important what form this finally takes—the physical sacrifice of one's life by a bodily death, the surrender of one's whole existence to Christ by vowing to live according to his commands, or by dying to the world in baptism together with Jesus in such a way that this death and resurrection may truly enable one to live one's life for the sake of that other, immortal life (cf. Rom 6:12ff.). Man becomes aware of the nature of his particular mission in life when he calmly puts his trust in God. But whatever particular Christian state the believer may live in, he lives as one who has died and been resurrected, because his whole existence is an attempt to make a loving and thankful response to God "by faith in the Son of God, who loved me and gave himself for me" (Gal 2:20).

This new edition furnishes an opportunity to make mention of a few difficulties and misunderstandings.

1. Should martyrdom be presented as a proof for the truth of the Christian faith? Yet how many have laid down their lives willingly or under coercion for quite different ideals! This is certainly true, and we owe our admiration to everyone who voluntarily and without fanaticism has dared to make his existence the burning torch for a pressing imperative of mankind, even if the program for which men and live and die are diverse and mutually opposed. Our concern was not the ethical earnestness of a given testimony and commitment, but (see my Preface) an interior criterion whereby the individual, interrupting for a moment his exegetical studies or projects for improving the world, could have judged whether or not he had taken the leap. One can die for various causes. But to die for love of the One who died for me in divine darkness: this face-to-face encounter is one of a kind, and it characterizes (this is the thesis of the book) the uniqueness of Christian truth and exis-

Translated by Adrian Walker.

tence. Thomas Aquinas says it in his own way when
he answers the question whether martyrdom is the
actus maximae perfectionis. The mere act of dying, he
affirms, is not, but if one considers the motive,
namely, *amor caritatis*, then "of all virtuous acts, blood
witness is the greatest proof of the perfection of love"
(*ST* 2.2.3c). And Kierkegaard knows this even better:
in the diaries of the last year of his life, he describes
much more dramatically everything I have attempted
to say.

2. Yet I must almost fear that the question raised
in *The Moment of Christian Witness* comes too late.
The serious young Christians and theologians for
whom this question was supposed to be an occasion
for reflection seem to be in large part already beyond
it. "Personally", a very gifted young theologian
writes me, "I have no fixed opinion on these issues. I
simply don't know 'how historical' the historical Jesus has to be for me to go on being or being able to
be a Christian. I try to keep a very open mind . . ."
An excellent attitude, but what will become of this
openness when one has to confess the faith *hic et
nunc*? Of course, the external obligation to decide is
not going to solve internal exegetical problems. But
it will perhaps place one terribly close, existentially,
to Paul and the others who, at the moment when
everything was on trial, were aware that they were
risking infinitely less than what God staked on their
behalf in his Son. If Christ had not suffered for

men—so argues Irenaeus against the Gnostics (and what else is the resolution of the bloody Cross into a "word event" but a form of Gnosis?)—"how then could he have called upon his disciples to take up their cross and follow him? That he said this not of the 'knowledge of the higher cross', as some do not blush to interpret it, but of the very suffering that he was to endure and that also awaited his disciples, he shows in the words: *he who secures his life will lose it . . .*" (*C. Haer.* 3:18.5). We have the right and the duty to investigate in ever-new ways and with ever-better methods the relationship of the apostolic kerygma to the historical basis it presupposes. Nevertheless, two pertinent facts must not be disregarded: (1) that precisely in relation to Jesus, historical-critical methods are a two-edged sword that can always be turned either to the right or to the left, depending on whether one has decided for or against faith in Christ; and (2) that in any case there are—in the order of magnitude made up of those historical figures among whom Jesus belongs as the founder of Christianity—certain "self-evident proofs" of quality (as W. Pannenberg says regarding the "sufficient self-demonstration of God in Christ" [1]), just as great works of art are never patched together out of "influences", just as prime numbers are indivisible.

3. But it must have been clear to every perceptive

[1] "Dogmatische Thesen zur Lehre von der Offenbarung", *Offenbarung als Geschichte* (2nd ed., 1963), p. 114.

reader of this little volume that I neither wanted nor was able to deal thematically with any exegetical problem in its pages.[2] The rapid enumeration of such problems (from a bird's-eye perspective) was, in fact, designed solely to review synthetically the allegedly valid exegetical reasons for postponing the decision of faith. Perhaps I will soon be permitted, *Deo volente*, to submit to the public the method I envision for approaching these questions correctly in a "Theology of the Old and New Covenants". Until then I would at least like to ask the reader to take the not-at-all exegetical but theological manifesto *Glaubhaft ist nür Liebe* (1963; Eng. ed. *Love Alone*) into consideration as the background of *The Moment of Christian Witness*.

4. Many have asked me sadly whether it was really necessary to attack so deserving a man as Karl Rahner. I have never made a secret of my admiration for the speculative power and the courage of Rahner,[3] and in difficult moment I have done my best to defend him,[4] but even early on I did not suppress certain doubts,[5] inasmuch as his choice of German Idealism as a point of departure seemed to me not

[2] Unfortunately, therefore, I can hardly concede the title of "perceptive reader" to the reviewer in *Orientierung* 15 (Dec. 31, 1966), who hunted *exclusively* for the solution to exegetical problems.

[3] "Christl. Kultur", supplement to *Neue Zürcher Nachrichten* (1964), no. 9.

[4] *Wort und Wahrheit* (1955), pp. 531–33.

[5] See my review of Rahner's *Geist in Welt* in the *Zeitschrift für katholische Theologie* (Innsbruck, 1939), pp. 371–79.

without danger. But to develop these reservations would mean reviving the whole debate about the legitimacy of Maréchal's interpretation of Thomas—the transposition back and forth between Thomas and a reading of Kant in the direction of Fichte—a dispute whose interest has faded today before the challenge to confront what remains valid in Thomas with that Hegel whom Feuerbach and Marx interpreted as the key of the contemporary technological world. Even J. B. Metz, Rahner's most authoritative disciple (to whom Rahner entrusted reworking the principal work of his earlier period), has resolutely gone beyond his master here; and, among others, Gustav Siewerth in particular has stigmatized the entire interpretation of Thomas advanced by Maréchal's school as an erroneous path, in his passionate work *Das Schicksal der Metaphysik von Thomas zu Heidegger* (Johannes Verlag: Einsiedeln, 1959). We shall not enter into this whole complex of problems here; it suffices to point out that the Maréchalian and Rahnerian interpretation of Thomas' "excessus" as the dynamism of the *affirmation ontologique* hardly does justice to the texts and above all considerably fails to capture the Thomistic understanding of *esse*. In contrast, intersubjectivity—newly discovered by Feuerbach (in the wake of Hegel) and fully exploited by Metz—the encounter between I and Thou, or personal love, plays the decisive role in the "precomprehension" of Christian revelation.

In addition, there is the fact that Karl Rahner, in his bold but often one-sided proposals, which are not always coordinated among themselves (there are many Karl Rahners!), often had to suffer the fate of the sorcerer's apprentice who was no longer able to exorcise from his disciples the spirits he had conjured up. Many of the more recent directions in his thinking are inspired by apostolic motives and, in Rahner himself, are still surrounded by a protective screen of theology (for example, the whole theory of the "anonymous Christian" based on the supernatural existential), but they immediately excite careless interpretations, which have also just as quickly made their appearance among disciples of a radical bent.[6] Who does not appeal to Rahner today more or less in this fashion when it is a question of some liberal broadening of dogma, of some transformation of its content into a "non-objective" reality, into something expressed only indirectly, or, in any case, something eminently capable of alteration!

If I cited Rahner's ideas and statements above all, it was because of their world-wide diffusion. On the other hand, the epigraph from Pascal (p. 77) was intended as a reminder that measurement against the origin is always necessary for Christians: in his Letter 3, Pascal called the Jesuits of his time back to their ori-

---

[6] One example among others is the book by H. R. Schlette, *Die Religionen als Thema der Theologie: Überlegungen zu einer "Theologie der Religionen"*, in the series *Quaestiones disputatae*, vol. 22 (Herder, 1964).

gin, Ignatius (not demythologized!), whose whole
foundation is a theology of the Cross transposed into
life. And I would like to take this opportunity to beg
the reader to consider further that everything the
Church has canonized (elevated to a standard rule) in
two thousand years as sanctity according to the measure of the Gospel corresponds unequivocally to the
criterion proposed in *The Moment of Christian Witness*:
every saint has attempted to shape his life into a loving
response to the crucified trinitarian love of God and
thus placed himself at the disposition of Jesus' work of
establishing God's kingdom of love among men. The
attempt to *reduce* religion to ethics, love of God and
personal love for Christ to love of neighbor, contra-
dicts so radically the Church's entire canon of sanctity
that one would have to contrast it sharply with the
tradition and dub it, say, "Neocatholicism".

5. In his unfailingly irenic manner and Christian
wisdom, Henri de Lubac has placed himself as a
peacemaker between the contesting parties in his essay
"The Religions of Man according to the Fathers",[7]
where he advances a proposal for reconciliation that,
it seems to me, does justice to both sides, not only ex-
teriorly and semantically, but at the depth of their
thought. He distinguishes in the Fathers a strict judgment on the individual mythical religions then known
to them and a much milder judgment on the religious

[7] "Les Religions humaines d'après les Pères", in *Paradoxe et Mystère de
l'Eglise* (Aubier, 1967), pp. 120–63.

phenomenon of humanity in general, a phenomenon
destined by Providence to find its transcendent fulfillment in Christianity. "The Church must, in the
opinion of the Fathers, integrate into its faith in Christ
the whole religious effort of humanity by converting
it. Such an integration displays two aspects, which
mutually imply each other: an aspect of purification,
even of battle and elimination (for everything is at first
more or less intermixed with error and evil); and an
aspect of assumption, assimilation and transfiguration
. . ." (p. 130). "Consequently, the definitive judgment
of the Fathers regarding the religious phenomenon—
so far as this judgment can be crystallized out of a mass
of texts and attitudes—is, . . . so to speak, a *dynamic*
judgment. It is formulated in the direction of the one
Church of Christ, the bearer of the absoluteness of
Christ. . . . Even less can other religions, whatever
merits they might possess, be regarded as 'salvific', that
is, enter or remain in 'competition' with faith in
Christ . . . ." Our task is "in no wise to make *static*
judgments regarding different religious situations, or
to compare the diverse religious systems with one another . . . as if it were a matter either of condemning
them or of admitting that certain of them could in
themselves constitute 'economies of salvation' established by God—whether one terms them 'extraordi-
nary' or 'ordinary'. . . . To arrange diverse religious
systems side by side is to assume the possibility that
they all come equally from God . . . even though they

indicate not only different but divergent ways . . ."
(pp. 132–34). Together with Teilhard de Chardin, we
must maintain faith in the "uniqueness of the axis", in
that "draining and unifying energy" which centers all
of humanity's sacred and secular history in Christ and
his Church. We must also, Henri de Lubac tells us,
avoid "separating the two sides that can be distin-
guished in Jesus' work, that of teacher and that of sav-
ior": "In Jesus, it is the same man who teaches and
dies. . . . The one who sacrifices himself for all is also
the one who demands an unconditional adherence to
his teaching and his person." His revelation is a no less
thoroughly new reality than the act of his redemptive
death. Yet this novelty does not prevent Christ's grace
from operating outside of the visible Church: "No
Christian would deny that in the various milieux of
life and culture there are 'anonymous Christians' who
in one way or another have received insights originating from the Gospel. . . . But it would be a fallacy to
conclude from this that there is an 'anonymous Christianity' spread everywhere in humanity, a so-called
'implicit Christianity', which the apostolic preaching
would have the sole task of bringing . . . to the state
of explicitness—as if the revelation brought by Christ
had done nothing except bring clearly to light what
had already always been universally present" (pp. 150–
53), as if "everything were reduced to the communication of a few formulas without renovating power, a
sort of label glued onto a container whose unchanged

content we always possessed 'anonymously' " (p. 152). De Lubac's illuminating distinction between "anonymous Christian" (as long as this expression is not stretched too far!) and "anonymous Christianity" does full justice to the exigencies of the present hour: on the one hand, to the certainty that the herald of the Christian Gospel does not enter into a zone entirely deprived of grace (since Christ died for all); on the other hand, to the most urgent summons to bear witness with our whole existence to the peerless grace that God has shown toward us in his Son.[8] But let us turn to the last objections:

6. The book has been reproached for sarcasm. Sarcasm is the dominant tone in many passages, but not in those where it is a question of the holy and glorious matter itself. It is my opinion that the prophets and Paul teach us to use this stylistic device as the right method of treatment in certain cases.

7. *The Moment of Christian Witness*, with its allusion to blood-witness, was nothing but a danger signal: the situation of the Church today is bloody earnest! We are busily engaged at the moment in sketching—like an exercise in freehand drawing—the whole gamut of possible new Christianities, which threaten to lose every continuity with what until now was un-

---

[8] I hope that Fr. Malevez, who would like to retain the expression "anonymous Christianity"—see his review of *The Moment of Christian Witness* in *NRTh* (Louvain, 1967): 1107)—can also agree with Henri de Lubac's unifying proposal.

derstood as Christianity, and which would perhaps do better to change their trademark. Yet the present situation is such that mere official calls for obedience will hardly do anything to change it; indeed, in many circles, people would—instead of withdrawing, like the Jansenists, into "reverent silence"—gaily laugh such decrees in the face. On the other hand, everything must be done to prevent an emigration of the progressivists, however uncomfortable their continued presence in the Church will prove to be for the faithful. What, pray tell, is the attitude the Christian is supposed to take during a homily that enlightens him as to the fact that Incarnation, Cross, resurrection, ascension, Pentecost are nothing but mythical-metaphorical ways of clothing the message, permitted in the past by God in view of the times, whereas today they are to be replaced by quite different modes of expression?[9] I ask the bishops: Is the hearer of such a homily dispensed from Mass? *May* he, *ought* he perhaps leave this liturgy?

But such an approach is out of the question for the Catholica, just as is a secession of the Neocatholics, which would have the effect of once more hurling the remnant back into lifeless, cheerless integralisms.

8. The solution to which some openly and shamelessly invite us in these difficulties is that of a pluralism of opinion within the substance of dogma. After

[9] See, for example, H. R. Schlette, "Einheit im Osterglauben?", in *Kirche unterwegs* (1966): 118.

all, pluralism is *the* watchword for the Church in the world—why should it be any different on the inside of the Church? "Is Christ risen?" "Now, don't get excited: it all depends on how you look at it. Analogously, symbolically, he certainly is." And if the expression "pluralism" should (for the time being) appear too daring within the compass of the truth of faith, one can, of course, always distinguish between the content of faith and the verbal form of expressing it: Isn't it true that no formulation captures the mystery? Hence, I always have the right to get an entirely different idea out of the same formulas: how many different meanings "person" has, how many "nature"! The form of the Catholic Church would thereby be completely assimilated to that of Protestantism: the same name, the same church building and liturgy join the so-called orthodox with the so-called liberals—if these distinctions still have any meaning in the post-Bultmann era. Should this characterize the actual situation of the Catholic Church, she would—and this is going to be very difficult to do—have to bear this situation out to the end without being able to accept it. But what she would then need in order to master such a superhuman task would not be merely theologians (that too), but, in plain terms, saints. Not mere decrees, much less the institution of new study commissions, but saintly figures to serve as beacons by which we can find our bearings. And that was ultimately the objective of the emergency call in *The Moment of Christian Witness*. It is not true that we can do nothing to get saints. For example, we ought at least to try, though a bit belatedly, to become something like them ourselves. "Better late than never."